With Warm Regards,

[signature]

A Labor Viewpoint:
ANOTHER OPINION

A Labor Viewpoint:
ANOTHER

OPINION
by
SOL CHICK CHAIKIN

Foreword by
Senator Daniel Patrick Moynihan

1980 LIBRARY RESEARCH ASSOCIATES
MONROE, NEW YORK

©1980 SOL CHICK CHAIKIN

All rights reserved.
This book, or parts thereof, must not be reproduced in any form without permission of the publishers, except for short phrases used in review.

PRINTED IN THE UNITED STATES OF AMERICA.

LIBRARY RESEARCH ASSOCIATES,
DUNDERBERG ROAD, MONROE, NEW YORK 10950

BOOK AND COVER DESIGN:
JANET SCHWERDT HACK © CREATIVE IMAGE, WARWICK, N.Y. 10990

Photo on back cover © Karsh, Ottawa

Library of Congress Cataloging in Publication Data
Chaikin, Sol Chick
A Labor Viewpoint: Another Opinion
Includes index.
1. Foreign trade and employment—United States. 2. International Ladies' Garment Workers' Union. 3. Clothing trade—United States. 4. Trade-unions and foreign policy—United States. I. Title.
HD5718.C62U53   338.4'7687'0973
80-12784   ISBN 0-912526-26-2 (pbk.)

A Labor Viewpoint:

ANOTHER OPINION

by
SOL CHICK CHAIKIN

Editors
Ethel Grodzins Romm
Rosalind Bryon Chaikin

DEDICATION

To this union upon which millions of garment workers have relied for a better opportunity for themselves and their children;

To the tens of thousands of dedicated full-time officers and rank and file leaders whose personal dedication and sacrifice over the past 80 years have served to sustain the membership and the union organization;

To my wife Rosalind who has shared with me the traumas and despair of disappointment and defeat and made the rare successes so exhilarating. These efforts of mine over the past many years could not have been sustained without her support. This very work was inspired by her.

Sol Chick Chaikin

TABLE OF CONTENTS:

part One
THE MYTH OF FREE TRADE

Foreword	Senator Daniel Patrick Moynihan	i
Introduction		v
one	Free Trade Or Fair Trade	3
two	A Tale Of Two Bras	19
three	Crying In The Washington Wilderness	25
	A. A Tale Of Many Cities	27
	B. Unraveling A Union	31
four	Importing Mexico's Unemployment	37
five	We Have So Much In Common, America And Britain	45
six	The Labor Summit, Tokyo, 1979	51
seven	Best Of A Bad Bargain	61
eight	Coping With A Changed World	75

part **Two**

SOCIAL UNIONISM

one	Organized Labor: Its Historic Role	93
two	ILG: A Special Union In A Unique Industry	103
three	The Two-Tier Society Of The United States	115
	A. Our Two-Tier Labor Force	115
	B. Our Two-Tier Employers	119
	C. Our Working Poor: We Must Do Better	121
	D. Collective Bargaining Issues In The 1980s	124
four	The Constant Struggle	135
	A. "Always Look For The Union Label."	135
	B. "Right To Work" Or "Right To Work For Less"?	138
	C. Industrial Citizen: Organizing The Unorganized	140

Table of Contents:

    D. Political Citizen: Politics Is
       Everybody's Business   146

    E. Our Own Third World:
       Immigration As A Dilemma For
       U.S. Trade Unionists   148

five   Human Rights: Where There Are No Free Trade Unions, There Are No Other Human Rights   155

    A. The United States Is
       Not An Island   155

    B. Exporting Democracy   158

    C. The Belgrade Incident   161

    D. The U.S. And Britain Share A
       Commitment   170

    E. A Chilean Chronical   171

    F. Statement In Japan On The
       Indo-Chinese Refugees   180

    G. A Clarion Call From
       The White House   181

part **Three**

PULLING TOGETHER: AN AGENDA FOR AMERICA

one	A.	We Face Complex Challenges	187
	B.	Unemployment/Full Employment	190
	C.	The Scourge of Inflation	194
	D.	Energy: Engine of Inflation	200
	E.	New Labor Legislation: Doesn't Labor Deserve An Even Break?	203
	F.	Tax Justice and the Inequitable Distribution of Wealth	205
	G.	Military Strength: Might Not Myth	207
	H.	Labor is All Out For the Equal Rights Amendment	210
two		Corporate Responsibility	215
End Note			223
Acknowledgements			225
Index			227

Table of Contents:

FOREWORD

Ask Americans if this country is different and they will tell you it is and they will be right.

Press on. Ask in what ways we are different. Again you will get sound answers. We are a people shaped by the frontier; a land of opportunity for all; a government conceived in liberty; an economic system based on freedom of contract and enterprise. All this and more will be said, and it, too, will be true.

But inexplicably, when we think of the great institutions of American society, the one we most often overlook is the most singular of all, the American labor movement. It is an ancient institution, as ours go. (If I were to have these observations printed in tomorrow's *Congressional Record* they would be set in type by members of the Columbia local of the International Typographical Union organized here in Washington in 1815.)

It is a surpassingly stable institution. When George Meany died in 1980, the AFL-CIO, which is to me the National Federation of Trade Unions, could trace its history back 99 years. During that time there had been nineteen Presidents of the United States; but just four presidents of the labor movement, and of these one served for a single year. It is a movement utterly committed to democratic government both in this nation and elsewhere in the world. (I once served as Ambassador to India. I could count on seeing one Senator in two years, two Congressmen in one. But hardly a month went by without someone from the AFL-CIO coming through New Delhi on some fraternal visit or other.) And it is a movement wholly committed to private enterprise in the United States. In this it is truly singular. With the practical exception of the trade unions of Canada, many of which are North American organizations that operate in both countries, giving rise to titles such as the *International*

Ladies' Garment Workers' Union, most trade unions in the democratic nations are more or less committed to public ownership, or at least public direction, of industry. And, of course, the only places you will find trade unions, real trade unions, are in democracies.

The American commitment goes back to the late 19th century, to the days of Samuel Gompers, his colleague Peter McGuire, and the others, mostly New York City workers who founded the American Federation of Labor. They, too, were tugged in the direction of their European counterparts. But they resisted. Instead they offered a different set of terms by which organized workers would deal with their employers and the society at large. I have termed this a "social contract," and I believe that it has been the basis of much of the social stability and progress of the modern era of American democracy. Its terms were simple and direct:

- First, labor would not seek to transform the American economic system by posing an alternative system.
- Second, labor would not seek to transform the American political system by founding its own political party.
- But, third, in return, the labor movement would not only be permitted but would be encouraged to seek to gain within the American system so constituted a broad range of material and social benefits for the people it represented.

One would search long and hard through the political history of this century to find a broad social agreement that has been so honorably and scrupulously upheld as American labor's adherence to that social contract.

Labor's choice was right. The political and economic stability which that agreement fostered, and the gains won by labor under it, in turn brought unequaled well-being, dignity, and position to American workers.

And yet, as Derek C. Bok and John T. Dunlop observe in their study, *Labor and the American Community,* "unions are among the least understood of our social institutions." The more then can we welcome this superbly informative collection of essays by Sol C. Chaikin, one of our most distinguished trade union leaders. "Chick" Chaikin, as he has been known since long before his Air Force days in World War II, is a man of extraordinary breadth of interests and depth of commitment. He is, moreover, head of a no less extraordinary union, the ILGWU. The history of trade unionism is not different from that of most social or political movements. The better off, more skilled workers were the first to organize. (Those printers here in Washington, for example.) The task of extending organization to the least skilled, and lowest-paid workers has called for the greatest talents and energies. Happily, this challenge has been met through three generations of leadership by the "ILG."

Chick writes about this, and more, with eloquence, insight, intelligence and the compassion of a person responsible for the well-being of over 350,000 workers. He knows for whom he speaks and why.

Possessed of a natural talent to exhort, to elucidate, to enliven, his time has been filled with speaking engagements before all kinds of groups—from the highest councils of our government to international conferences, academic seminars, political rallies and union meetings.

Twenty-seven of his most luminous papers have now been transcribed, edited, and arranged. The resulting volume is a most welcome and exceptionally valuable addition to labor history, to our understanding of the American trade union as an institution, and to the unique problems which face the unions of the garment and apparel industry.

Senator Daniel Patrick Moynihan
Washington, D.C., March 9, 1980

INTRODUCTION

Sol Chick Chaikin was elected president of the International Ladies' Garment Workers' Union in the summer of 1975, during the deepest recession in the United States since the great depression of 1929. It was a grim period in the union's long history, not only because of hard times but because the future looked bleak.

Since its founding in 1900, the ILG, as it is usually called, had faced other hard times—bankruptcy, betrayal, recession, troubles of many kinds—but never hopelessness. Now garments made in the almost no-wage countries of the Third World were flooding the U.S. market. Union membership had fallen from 457,000 in 1969 to below 1946 levels, a loss of 80,000 members and their job opportunities. The hard-won membership gains of decades were being wiped out. At best the future looked dark as more and more imports were permitted entry.

Most commentators were not at all concerned with these events. The U.S. garment industry was doomed, said most economists, and properly so. Let low-wage foreign populations produce clothes cheaply and let U.S. garment workers transfer to hi-tech jobs paying better wages. A pretty theory it was, but there were no such jobs. During the 1970s, everything from 100 percent of the colored TV sets to 20 percent of the cars were being made abroad. While the U.S. work force increased by 5 million jobs in the service sector, the number of industrial jobs fell by a half-million. The textile and apparel industry, which historically has been the source for 1 out of 8 U.S. industrial jobs, lost 200,000 of them by 1980.

The ILG's trauma was to be the bellweather for many other industries, but the early warning signals were invisible to most Americans. As the 1970s began, garment factories, averaging only 50 production workers per plant, were closing in towns across the country; a few hundred were thrown out of work here, a few dozen there, adding up to tens of thousands unemployed with no opportunity for other work. But no single event created enough drama to warrant coverage on the 7 o'clock news. By the end of the decade, when 13,000 steel workers were suddenly laid off by one corporation, the country had a televised example of the effects both of imports deluging the U.S. market and of corporate money fleeing it.

The record of Chaikin's response to the nation's growing but hidden crisis is contained in his speeches, press conferences and congressional testimony. He spoke from a prestigious platform. The ILG, through its remarkable president of 34 years, David Dubinsky, had grown influential beyond its numbers. It was a potent force in the politics of New York City and state, with White House connections through every president since Franklin Roosevelt. As the union that operated within the largest single manufacturing industry in New York, it commanded attention.

Chaikin broadened the union's audience. His mission: to present "another opinion" against the tide of conventional wisdom. The groups he addressed were often congregations of powerful people, such as the Trilateral Commission, the Council on Foreign Relations, the Council on Economic Development, executive seminars at the Harvard Center for International Affairs and the Columbia Graduate School of Business.

This book includes speeches, excerpts from speeches and congressional testimony from 1973 to early 1980, not in chronological order but by issues. Part I, "The Myth of Free Trade," analyzes the consequences of misunderstanding the world's economic disorders, and of permitting imports to capture each year an additional 6 percent and more of a U.S. market growing at less than 3 percent annually. Part II, "Social Unionism," proposes ways to make capitalism in the United States "more populist and more just." Part III,

"Pulling Together: An Agenda for America," discusses the twin evils of unemployment and inflation and suggests approaches and responses to those and other traumas of our times.

The book by necessity lacks one important element: a recording of a speech. The spoken word, edited for reading, cannot duplicate the power of oratory. In top form, Chaikin is a gripping, charismatic speaker. The reader who tries reading passages aloud will often be rewarded, in the midst of a discussion on the causes of unemployment, with the cadence of free verse. Perhaps the most moving ideas are in the chapter on human rights ("Where There Are No Free Trade Unions There Are No Other Human Rights"). Among the extraordinary documents is the transcript of a press conference in Chile where Chaikin, as a vice-president of the AFL-CIO, reports to Chileans on his meeting with the right-wing dictator General Pinochet to argue against the repression of Chilean free trade unionists. Another is a statement he made as a "public member" delegate appointed by President Carter to the Belgrade Conference, which lambastes the Soviet regime for not permitting invited U.S.S.R. citizens, Andrei Sakharov among them, to attend an AFL-CIO convention. The material describes practical but rarely discussed ways to "export U.S. democracy."

Chick Chaikin has a gift for clarifying complex issues. The analysis of Big Business/Big Labor and Little Business/Little Labor, or what Chaikin calls the Two-Tier U.S. system, provides a map of economic U.S.A. for guidance through otherwise mysterious, apparently chaotic national and international events. The reader comes away with a clearer idea of how political changes come about, with an understanding of economics such that foreign news and business pages begin to make more sense, and with an insight into the U.S. labor movement enough to unsettle the strongest stereotypes.

Ethel Grodzins Romm

part **one**

THE MYTH OF FREE TRADE

The countries of the world are now so tied together economically that national policies have global consequences. All of our own efforts at trade negotiations have been directed in the name of "free trade," a slogan from the 1930s that masks this radically changed nature of the world. Other countries are not free trading zones for our goods, yet they all come knocking at our doors demanding instant entry, and we try to oblige. As a direct result, serious damage is being done to the industrial fabric of our country. Until recently there has been inadequate representation of another point of view. I want to articulate that other viewpoint here.

Sol Chick Chaikin

one

Free Trade Or Fair Trade

To members of the International Ladies' Garment Workers' Union at Unity House, the union's worker resort in the Pennsylvania Poconos, May 15, 1979.

Why are we encountering so much difficulty in convincing our opinion leaders that the trade policies of the United States are disastrous? Why is it so difficult to persuade them that we must rationalize our trade policies, fairly and humanely?

After World War II no one foresaw the coming miracle of German and Japanese economic recovery or the push of the desperately poor nations to industrialize. The rules governing what little trade there was were set in 1947 by GATT, the General Agreement on Tariffs and Trade, and they were mainly about lowering tariffs. The United States then was not a trading nation. Imports came to a mere 3.5 percent of our gross national product, exports to only 8.5 percent.

Everyone had learned, we were told, the secret of avoiding another 1930s depression. Conventional wisdom held that one villain alone had been largely responsible for the world-wide depression of the 1930s, the flowering of fascism, the rise of nazism, the spread of communism, and ultimately World War II, and that was a high tariff wall around each country, preventing the free flow of trade.

So simple a remedy to cure so many ills is rarely found and, once found, is reluctantly abandoned. The GATT rules fell apart in the changed world of the 1960s, forcing a new set of global negotiations in the Tokyo Round of 1973. Textiles had been a special and separate problem and various cotton and multifiber agreements were made. But the best and the brightest in the United States have always been convinced that tariff walls built high around America would in the end be disastrous for Americans.

Never mind that the rest of the world is becoming walled off to American-made goods, if not by overt tariffs then by covert rules and regulations. No matter that the American consumer gains little price advantage with most imported goods. They are rarely bargains because their prices are raised to domestic levels, and whether a bra was made in Mexico or the United States, it costs the consumer the same amount. No matter that sometimes the imported price is higher than the domestic one. Never mind that thousands upon thousands of Americans are out of work. Since World War II, a low tariff system has been idealized by Americans of every political stripe.

So I've been out talking to every kind of group willing to listen to me. I seek the widest possible audience because we in labor need allies. We need to alert voters, legislators and government officials to the dangers that threaten American workers.

Trilateral Commission,
Washington, D.C., June 11, 1978.

To help change American public opinion about the impact of imports, Chaikin, upon his election as president of the ILGWU, began to accept invitations ranging far outside the usual circles that labor leaders generally confront.

Probably no organization in America is more filled with leaders and opinion makers than the Trilateral Commission. Sometimes called "the international brain trust" by the press, the Commission is, by its own description, a "private North American, West European, Japanese initiative on matters of common concern . . . a very select membership . . ., now about 250." Its membership is comprised of academicians, management representatives, financial experts, labor leaders, members of Congress and others from western industrialized nations, including Japan.

Its North American chairman, one of three, is David Rockefeller, Chairman of Chase Manhattan Bank, who helped found it in July 1973 to bring together "countries from the three areas which are the core democratic industrial regions with about 75 percent of the GNP [Gross National Product] of the non-Communist world."

Its former director was Zbigniew Brzezinski, now Assistant to the President for National Security Affairs. Jimmy Carter as well as Walter Mondale were members before their election as President and Vice President made them ineligible for continued participation.

Chaikin, himself a member of the Trilateral Commission since 1977, shared the platform with Rep. John Anderson, Chairman of the House Republican Conference, and Anthony Solomon, Under Secretary of the Treasury for Monetary Affairs. The morning's topic was, "The Domestic Setting of American Foreign Policy-Making."

It is natural to assume that when the president of the Ladies' Garment Workers' Union argues for regulation of apparel imports, he is indulging in egregious special pleading. I should like to confirm your suspicions at the outset and plead guilty. In addition, however, I will try to establish that the "fair trade" policies we in the ILG fight for are good not only for America's garment workers but also for the entire American economy.

It is my sworn responsibility to defend and protect the interests of some 400,000 garment workers in America, especially to safeguard their opportunities for employment. Let me draw a profile of our members. First, they cannot stand prolonged unemployment. Even when they work, their pay is relatively skimpy, in a sector of the economy where competition can still be cutthroat. Second, many are drawn from the marginal population of the nation—black, Hispanic, poor white, and recent immigrants. Third, they are 80 percent female who are most often heads of families. It would be a dereliction of duty if our union—or I, personally—were to stand by silently, watching thousands of their jobs wash away annually in a floodtide of imports. Therefore, we do plead for our people.

In doing so, we are mindful of the dictum of Hillel who said, "If I do not speak for myself, who will?" We are not, however, unmindful of his second dictum, "If I speak for myself alone, what am I?" If we in the ILGWU pleaded for garment workers alone, without regard to what happened to others, we would be doing what comes naturally, but not necessarily what is most socially responsible. Hence, in the pursuit of our self-interest—in truth, our survival—we have tried repeatedly to assess our role in the society as a whole, both America and the world.

What we have discovered is that our peculiar problem is not quite so parochial as we ourselves were inclined to believe. The threat to apparel-making is a threat—in greater or lesser measure—to similar labor-intensive, light manufacture in the United States, employing about one in ten American workers in some 10 million jobs. Moreover, the peril is now spreading to heavy capital-intensive manufacturing as well. This decline of American manufacture, under the twin assaults of commodity imports and capital exports, must lead inexorably to the decline of the service sector and thus to the shrinking of the total American economy.

This plague is wholly preventable. We must begin to cope sensibly with the realities of world trade in the last fifth of the twentieth century—realities now obscured under the heap of false dogmas still guiding our international economic moves.

For some two decades now, the leadership of our union has been prodded by circumstances into a highly instructive intellectual odyssey over stormy economic oceans. In the 1950s we saw some apparel jobs wiped out by a flood of silk scarves from Japan. Our first response was to minimize the unhappy event as too picayune to concern us in a booming industry within a bouncy economy. A few years later, however, the "dollar blouse" from Japan began to erode a larger sector of our industry, with other apparel lines visible on the import horizon. As the picayune became potent, we could no longer afford to be cavalier. We had to think, and we had to act.

How to act was not clear for a union such as ours, one steeped in an international outlook from the day its earliest founder heard the call, "Workers of the world, unite!" We were anti-protectionist in theory, but we were also pro-worker in principle and practice. To reconcile this clash of priorities, we used the sound pragmatic trade union approach. We urged a sort of collective bargaining with other nations at the international level.

We urged negotiated quotas, first with Japan and, step by step, with dozens of other nations under the current provisions of the various Multifiber Arrangements, designed to eliminate market disruption in importing countries. The basic concept was, and is, to agree upon levels of imports and exports that allow us Americans to live while permitting other nations to share our market. Under this concept, when the American market expands, both imports and domestic production can expand. Everyone should gain.

But, although such quotas have served a purpose, they are now being used to ruin us. In years when the United States market grew by only 2 or 3 percent, imports were allowed to expand by more than 6 percent annually, compounded. Through loopholes in the arrangements, such as allowing one year's quotas to be applied to another year, or allowing one product to be substituted for another, imports in some lines have grown 25 to 35 percent per year. Consequently, the quotas have become just a delaying action that only postpones the day of our death.

In 1966 there were 641,000 employees in women's apparel. By 1976 that number had shrunk to 591,000—a loss of 50,000 jobs in one decade. Behind this sinister story stands a causative statistic: in 1966, one garment out of every twelve was an import. Now it is one out of every three.

Although we in the ILG were keenly aware of the problem as it affected women's apparel, we soon found that the same calamity was threatening the entire textile and apparel industry, including men's clothing, and for the same reasons. Imports were eroding jobs by the tens of thousands in America's largest factory industry—textiles and apparel—an industry that employs one out of every eight manufacturing workers.

As we began to cry out for relief, we were advised by slide-rule-toting economists that there were two sure-fire ways to cope with the problem of imports: First, we should become more competitive, both wage-wise and production-wise; and second, we should encourage our people to find jobs in other sectors of the economy. Both suggestions were drawn from classical economic notions of "free trade" that assume an inevitable ultimate equilibrium—each country produces what it can turn out best and most cheaply for world sale while workers within countries merely move from one industry to another as their countries find their special thing to make for the international mart. Everyone gets bargains and everyone works.

Before applying ourselves to a theoretical analysis of these traditional tenets, however, consider a few of the facts that confronted us. The first fact was the disparity between wages here and in the lands that were exporting to us. While an American sewing machine operator earned about $3.00 an hour in 1975, workers doing the same job in Hong Kong received 62 cents an hour; in Korea and Singapore, 27 cents; and in Haiti, 18 cents. For American workers to "compete"—even at the low wage of garment workers in the industrial pecking order here—they would have to become five, ten, or fifteen times as productive as their overseas counterparts. We have no such bionic men and women in our shops.

If the hands of our workers could not be that many times more nimble than those of workers in other lands, why couldn't we compete by putting our highly touted American know-how to work, surely far superior to the primitive industries in Haiti, Singapore, and Korea? We soon discovered what Pogo discovered long before us: "We have met the enemy and they is us." We learned that a vast portion of overseas production is carried on by American methods, implanted by American companies. United States manufacturers and chain stores "contract" out garment manufacture to plants in other lands where the work is done with American techniques, design, and sizing and is backed up with American financing and merchandising skill. Indeed, the brand name of the U.S. company is stitched into the garment in the far-away factory.

Would you be surprised to learn that today the United States supplies many raw materials at the cheapest world prices? That is because of two major factors. First, the rate of inflation in low-wage countries overseas far exceeds our own and, second, the cost of the raw material in clothes made of polyester has gone up faster there, due largely to the higher cost of energy overseas. In spite of these advantages, nothing can offset a pay scale that ranges from one-quarter down to one-twelfth of ours.

Consequently, to expect the U.S. worker to "compete" is just so much empty exhortation. The only alternative would be to cut the U.S. wage to something like 75 cents an hour, a move that would not only make life intolerable for the individual workers but would, multiplied several million times over, destroy our American economy, dependent as it is upon a mass consumer market. No one earning 75 cents an hour in the United States can buy a bicycle, let alone a car, or a McDonald hamburger, never mind a steak. The high standard of living in the United States is due to the wages U.S. workers earn, which they quickly spend on products and services offered by their fellow Americans.

These facts, however, did not deter the classic "free traders" from continuing to manipulate their slide rules to match their jargon. If the United States' textile and apparel industry could not compete, then so be it, argued the technocrats. The displaced workers could find jobs in other trades, boots or shoes, or electronic assembly, or, they solemnly intoned, in other occupations where aptitudes were roughly comparable to those in textile and apparel. Yet, precisely because these proposed alternative industries were so comparable—labor-intensive, light product manufacture—they, too, were suffering from the same sickness we were.

American boot and shoe worker's jobs were being wiped out as Oriental, Brazilian, Spanish and Italian factories turned out footwear with American brand names on them. Radio assembly is totally foreign to the United States today, although we once had a thriving industry here. Black and white TV manufacture has left our land. Even color TV—our proud invention—has now lost its last American bastion as Zenith was forced to leave its native land under competition from others, like RCA, who exported production overseas.

Indeed, all labor-intensive manufacture in the United States has been hard hit: glass, rubber wear, metal fabrication, paper and wood products, ceramics, plastics, dolls, toys, novelties, cameras, bikes, furniture, cheap jewelry. Our displaced garment workers discovered that comparable employment was a cruel myth.

The next counsel we heard from "free traders" was to be broad-minded, open-hearted and far-sighted while our people, dispossessed from the labor-intensive sector, moved into the capital-intensive sector, industries like steel, auto, chemicals and computer technology. This advice was generally packaged in glossy language about how low-wage, labor-intensive industries fortunately no longer had a future in America. The current disturbances would only be temporary as our workers were absorbed by America's high-technology sectors, unrivaled by any country in the world.

This hypothesis, of course, purported to be pure Ricardo. The disciples of David Ricardo, the nineteenth century British economist, preached, you will recall, that by elevating ourselves to hi-tech jobs, we would be doing what we can do best—capital-intensive production—and we would surrender to the poor lands what they can do best—labor-intensive production. Thus would we all live in the best of all possible worlds.

When we gathered at our labor conventions, however, we found that our brethren in the steel industry were hurting—as badly as we were. In a decade, because foreign countries were permitted to dump steel here, the number of production workers employed in basic steel fell from 509,500 to 431,300. The unions representing workers in other heavy industries—like the International Association of Machinists—were objecting bitterly to the way corporations producing airplanes were closing shops here to open plants over there.

This destruction of high technology jobs was not supposed to be happening, according to the forecasts of the classic free traders. Two modern developments were at work to upset the classic free-trade hypothesis. First, many of the developed nations, like England, with a capacity for capital-intensive production, were subsidizing exports or permitting inflated prices in their domestic markets to allow their producers to "dump" on the American market. Here, I use the word "dump" in its standard sense, selling for export at prices below the domestic price or even below the cost of production.

The second factor, more important and more enduring, has been the export of capital, plants, technology, and managerial skills by U.S. multinational corporations to other lands. The movement has been massive and the motives have been many.

Many American corporations move production overseas because they cannot sell their U.S. made products overseas. While America is probably the most open of markets, a classic free-trade zone, the Common Market, Japan, Argentina, Australia, Brazil and all the Iron-Curtain countries make it difficult—sometimes impossible—for American-made wares to penetrate their high trade walls. Sometimes, our goods are excluded by tariffs; more often, the obstacles are thousands of bits and pieces of red tape that make entry impossible.

Many countries that should be hit with retaliatory measures are rewarded for their "protectionist," anti-free-trade policies. The reward is U.S. investment overseas. The forms of multinational operations are protean: wholly-owned subsidiaries, joint ventures, franchises, license, patents and the use of overseas producers as captive contractors for U.S. concerns.

The overseas investment offers a dual advantage to many corporations. They can sell abroad in a protected market, with high-profit prices set behind national walls, then use overseas production as a launching pad to export to the United States. Hence, many such corporations find themselves in a "sea captain's paradise" with one "protectionist" love over there and another love for "free trade" over here.

There are distinct tax incentives granted by our government to multinational corporations who manufacture in another land. Any profits realized in a foreign country are not taxable by the United States unless and until the profits are repatriated. Any taxes paid to a foreign government are allowed as a tax credit (worth at least twice as much as a tax deduction) when corporate income taxes are paid to Uncle Sam. Through a game called "transfer pricing," a corporation can have its subsidiaries bill one another in such a way as to show high profits in low-tax lands and no profits in high-tax lands so that, when all the bookkeeping is totaled, little or no taxes will be paid anywhere.

There are other tax advantages for those American companies who manufacture abroad. Our tax laws have sent our American capital, our American technology and our American management skills overseas faster than a speeding bullet.

This massive export of the factors of production makes the Ricardian tenet of "comparative advantage" a false dogma, inapplicable to the realities of today's world.

Our "advantages," we have been told, are threefold: our capital, our technology and our management skills. But when our money, our processes and our entrepreneurial know-how go overseas, the advantage becomes a disadvantage. Our own big guns are turned against us.

American manufacture, both light and heavy, both labor and capital intensive, is being deluged by the inflow of other people's commodities and the outflow of American capital. Between 1974 and 1977, the number of service-producing jobs in the nation rose by 4,600,000, while the number of jobs in American manufacture shrank by nearly 400,000.

It is this total rise in employment at a time when manufacture is shrinking that has given rise to another fashionable but false scenario for our future, a service economy without manufacturing. The rationale for this prospect has been our experience since the end of World War II. The service-producing sector has grown—at least in the number of its employees—from a minority to a majority position, now making up about 71 percent of the labor force. By simple extrapolation, the theoreticians predict that, in the foreseeable future, we ought to be able to make do with a service economy that supplies employment to 75 or 80 percent of the labor force, providing jobs for all those displaced in the industrial sector.

This Pollyanna forecast, however, pays no mind to the relationship between the commodity and service sectors of a society. Only as long as there is a powerful commodity foundation can there be a lofty service superstructure. For instance, when there are enough taxpayers, we can afford to have one out of six employees in the nation on government payrolls—as we do—and we can afford to have an expanding number of salespersons and repair people and personal service workers. But can we continue to maintain such a superstructure once we lose the 20 million jobs in American light and heavy industry? Taking in each other's wash is not the basis for a sound economy.

An imaginative variation on the theme of a service economy is the forecast that we will become a rentier nation, one living on its overseas investments. The sly strategem here is to live eternally with an adverse balance of trade as we go on buying more than we sell, then making up for those losses by returns on foreign investment to give us a tidy equilibrium—perhaps even a gain—in the balance of payments.

The consequences of such a policy do not have to be left to conjecture. We can learn much from the experience of Great Britain, which became a rentier economy at the turn of the century. British capital sought profits in overseas investments. Some 80 to 90 percent of investment was made abroad, leaving British manufacture in a state of pernicious capital anemia. Because its industry was neglected for at least three generations, Britain came out of World War II without any firm base for a viable economy. The mother of the industrial revolution now found herself in the deplorable state of some backward country, its prime minister declaring that the primary need of the United Kingdom was to "industrialize" its own impoverished islands.

A rentier economy in America would be a rerun of the British story: First, the nation divided as income from overseas flows into the pockets of a small elite while the great mass is low paid or out of work, dependent on the dole; second, a nation in profound distress without a commodity base to support those employed in commerce, trade, services, or government. A rentier economy must also assume that American investments overseas are, and always will be, safe, but how secure will they be in a world torn with national, tribal, and class conflict? In the long run, an American "empire," implied in a rentier economy, is likely to be as sound as the old British Empire.

Over the last few decades, we in the garment industry have

come to the conclusion that these attempts to apply the "free trade" policies of the past to the protectionist world of the present are bad not only for the garment industry, but also for the entire U.S. economy.

We are also increasingly persuaded that the exploitation of the poor in the Third World countries, using and abusing them to manufacture labor-intensive products for export to developed nations, has not proven to be in the best interest of either the nations or the workers who are seeking economic advancement. After two decades of development—based on a push for rapid industrialization—the masses in the poor countries are as poor as ever, even where there has been a growth in per-capita income.

During the 1960s, for instance, Brazil's GNP, the gross national product, per capita grew in real terms by 2.5 percent annually. However, the ratio of mean incomes of the upper 20 to the bottom 40 percent of the income-earning labor force was about nine to one in 1960 and twelve to one in 1970. The British publication, *The Economist*, noted in September 1974 that "in 42 other developing countries, the same trend tends to recur— an enlargement of economic income from the community as a whole with the benefits disturbingly concentrated at the richest end of the spectrum of income." While a "host country" may experience "high rates of growth," notes a United Nations report, "its income distribution may not improve or may even deteriorate....High income may accrue largely to domestic elites associated with foreign interest....Basic needs of the population, such as food, health, education and housing may be left unattended."

In sum, the present policies of "industrializing" the Third World turn out to be a process for enriching the rich in both the rich and poor countries, at the expense of the poor in both poor and rich countries.

What many Third World countries need first is an agriculturalization rather than an industrialization of their economies, since 50 to 80 percent of the populace of these lands is rural. What these populations can do best—to put the theory of comparative advantage to good use—is to grow food in their soils. If they were to concentrate on agriculture, the income of their farm families, which are the bulk of their people, would rise. Their families would probably be smaller and they could then comprise a domestic market for their own domestic manufacture as well as for imports.

Instead, the direction in the Third World has been to industrialize, which has had tragic consequences. Pinning their hopes on manufacture, these nations have neglected their agriculture. Way back in 1964, the U.S. Department of Agriculture researcher, Lester R. Brown, concluded that the less developed world was losing the capacity to feed itself. Up to 1940, these poor countries were all net exporters of wheat, rice and other grains to the more industrialized nations. By the end of World War II, this was turned around and the poor became net importers. Out of neglect, these countries were allowing their soils to become exhausted. Those in power depressed the prices of their farm produce within their own countries. As farm income sank, the poor families did what they do everywhere: they produced children as their best cash crop. Populations exploded as the arable soil shrank. Unable to live on the land, these desperate people poured into the cities to offer a cheap and ever cheaper labor supply. They offered their hands and their sweat in factories for pennies to produce products to be sold in other lands. The foreign exchange they were supposed to accumulate for their countries was insignificant. But the money they borrowed to import food was not insignificant. These nations would have done far better to raise and sell agricultural commodities.

The poor countries are now unable even to buy their needed food on the world market because they have become so deeply indebted they find it harder and harder to buy on credit. Meanwhile, the great suppliers of food products—the United States, Canada, Argentina and Australia—are finding it ever more difficult to supply the needed food products. Sterling Wortman, vice president of the Rockefeller Foundation, argues that there is still some hope for those countries that face devastating hunger if agrarian countries concentrate less on industry and more on agriculture. If in the poorer countries productivity and disposable income of large numbers of small farmers can be increased, markets will develop for imported food supplies and for products of urban industry. As fewer rural people feel the need to pour into the cities, the labor market will tighten and wages in the cities are likely to rise.

This means that there is no need for us to play the zero sum game in which we have to decide who shall go jobless and who shall go hungry in the world. If the Third World increases its agricultural output and its industrial production, there can be more for all in both the rich and poor lands. Standards of living can increase in both worlds. In such an expanding universe, international trade can continue as we share our growing market with other nations and as they—with newfound sources of wealth—share their markets with us.

The changed nature of world manufacture and trade since World War II makes touting assumptions from early nineteenth century free-trade theory a baleful indulgence. Equally harmful is the notion that poor lands will become rich lands through rapid industrialization financed with foreign capital to produce goods for sale back in the "mother" countries. Indeed, preaching such noxious fantasies serves to provide a rationale for the exploitation of working people in both developed and developing nations, and by precisely those corporations that once were the prime proponents of old-fashioned protectionism. Their dramatic conversion to "free trade" at home and to the once-forbidden industrialization of "backward" nations is based not on a devotion to either American consumers or Third World workers, but on a mindless pursuit of profits—mindless, I call it, for it is a drive made without regard even for its tragic consequences for American capitalism.

In contrast, we in the labor movement advocate policies that fit into none of the ethereal theories or precast patterns of the past. We propose programs that are based on the needs of our time, programs that will strengthen American capitalism and one of its handmaidens, a free and democratic trade union movement. Among our recommendations are these:

- Negotiate quotas with other nations based on a fair

and realistic sharing of markets.
- Remove non-tariff barriers that make a mockery of low-tariff schedules.
- Enforce anti-dumping provisions.
- Retaliate where other countries subsidize exports.
- Revise or repeal American tax laws that encourage overseas production.
- Repeal items 806 and 807 of the present U.S. tariff schedules that reward American companies for production abroad of products intended for sale in the United States.
- Regulate the export of American capital and technology.
- Offer technical aid to the developing nations to assist in their agricultural development.

These proposals do not exhaust the possibilities, but they do suggest that there are constructive alternatives to our present disastrous twin policies of "free trade" (but only here inside America) and rapid "industrialization" (but only for the Third World).

Let us take these steps swiftly.

(A shorter version appeared in USA Today *, Vol. 107 #2404, Jan. 1979, p. 17-20. Used by permission of the Society for the Advancement of Education.)*

A Tale Of Two Bras

General Executive Board, ILGWU,
Unity House, Pennsylvania, June 1975.

Because we can buy an occasional cheap blouse sewn in India or a discounted pair of pants stitched in Taiwan, American shoppers naturally assume that all products made overseas offer great bargains. We may experience some uneasiness when we learn the product has been made by someone who earns but 23 cents per hour [India] or 38 cents per hour [Taiwan], someone who may be forced to sweat twelve hours a day seven days a week, and who may even be only thirteen years old. Still, our money is worth less and less—the proof of our crippling inflation—and our first responsibilities are to our families.

Thus it comes as a double blow—to our pocketbooks and to our principles—to discover that we American consumers are usually no more the beneficiaries from overseas low wages than are the wretched souls who stitch there.

For the not-unexpected truth is that brand-name American manufacturers and buyers for our great retail stores buy cheaply abroad and then almost always jack up the prices to equal American-made goods. This is no more than we should expect of merchants whose first responsibility is to generate the highest possible profit. Thus the remedy must lie in legislation and regulation.

If there is a Santa Claus, Virginia, he is not making these bras.

These two bras were bought the same day in the same store. They're the same style, the same size, and made by the same company. Even the price is identical: $6.00.

The difference? Only this: One was made in the USA where the garment workers (lumping together union and non-union) average $3.57 an hour.

The other was made in Mexico where the garment workers average about 56 cents an hour. That's some difference.

Who got it?

Obviously, not the Mexican workers. Certainly not the American consumer.

Which makes you wonder about that old story you're always hearing: "If we make clothes in other countries where labor is cheap, the American consumer pays less." Some story.

If you bought the Mexican-made bra, an American garment worker was done out of work, a Mexican sweatshop was supported, and you got a bra at one heck of a mark-up.

Not to mention what it costs you in welfare payments and higher taxes and lost business when American workers can't get work.

Feeling had? Don't get mad, get even. Look for the union label.

Fair is fair.

International Ladies' Garment Workers' Union, 1710 Broadway, New York, N.Y. 10019.

From Justice, *the ILGWU newspaper*

Trade Subcommittee of the House Ways and Means Committee. Washington, D.C., March 25, 1976.

> The news about the illusory bargains in bras and other goods was greeted with some skepticism when the ILGWU first demonstrated it. Chaikin took the results of some comparison shopping in New Jersey, New York and Maryland to the Trade Subcommittee chaired by Representative William Green (D), Pa.
> The reader may wish to duplicate these findings. It is now nearly impossible, however, to buy a scarf, gloves, pocketbook, or a colored TV set for that matter, that has been made in the USA in order to make a comparison. These industries, and many others, scarcely exist in the United States any more.

SOL. C. CHAIKIN, President, International Ladies' Garment Workers' Union: Mr. Chairman, I have samples of identically-styled garments produced both in the United States and abroad, made of the same materials, but sold at the same prices to American consumers. This, I think, is part of an answer to a question asked by a member of your committee, Mr. Chairman, and I would like, with your permission, to offer them as exhibits.

WILLIAM J. GREEN: You may do so.

CHAIKIN: First, I offer three misses' shirts, style 1458, made of fabric blended from 65 percent acetate, 35 percent nylon, size 14. They are identified by a Sears Roebuck label and an RN number 43721 registered to Niki-Lu of Miami, Inc., according to information supplied by Mrs. Klein of the Federal Trade Commission on March 15, 1976. The three shirts were purchased from Sears at the Paramus Plaza, New Jersey, on March 13, 1976. The retail price is $8.00 each. One was made in the United States, one was assembled in El Salvador, and one in the Dominican Republic.

The detailed Sears sales slip shows the quantity purchased to be three, totaling $24.00. Stitch for stitch it is the same item, same quality, same piece goods, same style number, same Sears number, same Sears price for the people who would come in and buy.

Our second product consists of two brassieres, style No.

1038. The identification on these items is Warner's, RN 16396, one made in the United States, the other in Mexico, both purchased at Macy's on 34th St. in New York City on March 16, 1976. Their retail price was $6.50 each. The details of the Macy's sales slip are right here.

Our third product is a pair of Misses' blouses, style 46241, made of a knit fabric, otherwise not identified. That is just a small violation. They are identified as a product of White Stag, a large domestic company. One of the two garments was made in the USA and the other one in Japan, both purchased at Bloomingdale's on Lexington and 59th Streets in New York City on March 22, 1976. The retail price is $14 each. The details of the Bloomingdale's slip are right here.

These examples could have been multiplied by thousands of instances. Comparison shopping in men's clothing, conducted in several Baltimore stores, revealed the same pattern. *[See opposite]*

Baltimore, Md.
SHIRTS AT THE HECHT CO.

American-made—GOLDEN ARROW 100% polyester, button down, Short sleeve—$12

Imports—VAN HEUSEN Splendor Double knit, made in Taiwan 100% polyester
Long sleeve—$13
Short sleeve—$12

American-made—CLAY POOLE 3 button knit sport shirt 50% polyester, 50% cotton—$6.50

Imports—CLAY BROOK Made in Hong Kong 3 button knit sport shirts—$12.50

SHIRTS AT STEWARTS

American-made—ARROW Belmont short sleeve shirt—$9

Imports—VAN HEUSEN Van Luster, made in Taiwan Short sleeve shirt—$10

DENIM JACKETS AT THE HECHT CO.

American-made—LEE
$21.25 and $24

Imports—BRITANNIA SPORTSWEAR, Made in Hong Kong
$25, $27, and $27.50

JEANS AT THE HECHT CO.

American-made—LEE
$17

Imports—BRITANNIA SPORTSWEAR, Made in Hong Kong
$18 and $20

SWEATERS AT HUTZLER'S

American-made—ROBERT BRUCE, 100% Orlon acrylic—$20

Imports—the label read: MADE IN ITALY FOR HUTZ— LER'S 100% acrylic—$25

American-made—JANTZEN 100% Wintuck acrylic—$19 and $20

Samples collected by Martin Lesser, Upper South Department, International Ladies' Garment Workers' Union, on August 5, 1975.

three

Crying In The Washington Wilderness

Trade Policy Staff Committee,
Office of the Special Representative for Trade Negotiations,
July 21, 1975.

Beginning in the early 1960s, the ILGWU, foremost among a few other labor unions, had begun warning Congress of the consequences of its open-door, "free trade" policies in a closed-shut, locked-out trade world. Part of the problem was to explain the importance of labor-intensive work in America. As an example, here are the opening paragraphs of testimony given by Chaikin to the Trade Policy Staff Committee. These remarks were included in his "Statement on behalf of the International Ladies' Garment Workers' Union, AFL-CIO, in opposition to duty reductions on articles of women's and children's apparel."

The country was in the midst of a recession. Eight million people were out of work during the first half of this year, including a quarter of a million garment workers.

My name is Sol. C. Chaikin. I am President-Elect of the International Ladies' Garment Workers' Union, a labor organization affiliated with the AFL-CIO. I am appearing before you on behalf of more than 400,000 of our members in the United States and the Commonwealth of Puerto Rico who would normally be engaged in producing the various articles of women's and children's apparel if only there were sufficient work in their shops. I will seek to present their views to you about possible duty reductions on articles of women's and children's wear in the trade agreement negotiations authorized by the Trade Act of 1974. I am accompanied by our director of research, Dr. Lazare Teper.

It is indeed odd to talk about a possible reduction of customs duty on imported women's and children's wear at a time when unemployment among experienced garment workers in this country is as rampant as it has been this year.

The number of unemployed experienced garment workers averaged over one-quarter of a million men and women in the first half of 1975. These figures are, however, an understatement. They do not include workers in this industry, living in small towns and large, who have become discouraged because they cannot find work after long job searching. Such workers, who have stopped looking for work because work is unavailable, are no longer counted as "unemployed," but rather as "persons out of the labor force." With language, we magically shrink our unemployment figures.

Where are they to look for jobs when theirs is a one-industry town? Where are they to look if they live in a city where apparel provides the key source of employment for people of their skill and where unemployment generally is widespread and jobs of all kinds are lacking? Once there were shops which provided them with work making women's and children's wear. Now, in case after case, these shops either closed their doors or else drastically curtailed their work force. Many fortunate enough still to have jobs are forced to work on part-time schedules, even at the peak of season activity.

I am fully aware of the task faced by the Special Representative for Trade Negotiations during the forthcoming trade agreement talks, authorized by the Trade Act of 1974. I fully understand that you have to review the situation in all industries. I nonetheless appeal to you, with all the force at my command, not to permit tariff reductions on items of ladies' and children's apparel; for ours is not one of those industries where further duty cuts can be made without most serious injury to the industry and its workers and, thus, to the entire country.

        Chaikin and Teper appeared many times before many committees and began to attract the attention of some congressmen and congresswomen.

A.
A Tale Of Many Cities

Remarks from Executive Program in Business Administration, Columbia University at Arden House, August 17, 1977.

In the United States we have a careless view about high unemployment. At 5 percent it is an item of minor concern. At 7 percent we begin to view with alarm. At 8 percent panic begins to set in and at double digit unemployment, everybody begins to look for another candidate.

In Germany, where the social costs of unemployment were learned in the most brutal fashion during the 1930s, Ground Zero is 1 percent. When they reached 3.4 percent for a short while, it was a national tragedy and all forces were marshalled. With us 3.4 percent is barely Ground Zero.

The loss of traditional job opportunities and the failure to create new employment can creep up on us. When a single steel company in one fell swoop closed 15 plants and 13,000 employees were thrown out of work, headlines screamed. The hemorrhaging of jobs was obvious. In contrast, garment factories are small and usually individually owned. One shop closes down in Kentucky and 46 workers lose their jobs. Another closes up in Massachusetts with 143 and another in California with 61. They do not seem important, those little shops, but add up 46 plus 143 plus 61 plus all the other laid-off workers and it comes to 200,000 jobs lost in the textile and apparel industry, 200,000! For a decade or more we have been bleeding to death, silently, invisibly.

The following exerpts from the Congressional Record
tell the stories of some small towns in the United States.

Congressional Record

United States of America

PROCEEDINGS AND DEBATES OF THE 95th CONGRESS, FIRST SESSION

Vol. 123   WASHINGTON, TUESDAY, SEPTEMBER 27, 1977   *No. 152*

Mr. HUGHES. Mr. Speaker, I thank my distinguished colleague, the gentleman from South Carolina (Mr. Mann), for yielding.

Mr. Speaker, it is a long, long way from Geneva, Switzerland, to Egg Harbor, N.J. But I trust that our country's representatives who recently negotiated the renewal of the Multifiber Agreement at Geneva were aware of the impact of their activities on towns all over the United States like Egg Harbor. I say "towns like Egg Harbor," because for lots of people in Egg Harbor itself it is already too late.

Egg Harbor is a very small community. The Lisa Manufacturing Co., a garment firm, was one of its few employers. It employed 65 workers—not a large number by big city standards—but in a town the size of Egg Harbor it was one of the mainstays of the local economy. In January of this year the Lisa Manufacturing Co. closed its doors and went out of business—because it could no longer meet the challenge of cheap imports produced by workers in far-off countries who earn 30 and 40 cents an hour.

The loss of these 65 jobs has had a major, devastating effect on the economy of Egg Harbor. And a dozen miles up the road, in Hammonton, N.J., the situation was repeated when the Aggressive Coat Co. employer of some 90 workers, ended operations at about the same time. And in town after town from one end of the country to the other come similar stories—stories of small and medium-sized establishments, frequently the mainstay of a community's economy, closing down under the relentless pressure of low-wage foreign competition, leaving economic disaster and human misery in their wake.

The stories of the Egg Harbors and the Hammontons of America, small though the number of workers in each individual case may appear to be, add up. In my own State of New Jersey alone, for example, fully one-quarter of the jobs in the apparel industry have been lost during the last 10 years—and they have been lost very largely as a direct result of the import problem. In 1966, more than 80,000 New Jersey workers were employed in that industry. But by last year the number had shrunk to 60.000—and is still declining.

Job losses of this magnitude constitute a major dislocation of the economy of the communities involved and the state as a whole; but for the individuals involved and for their families they often constitute an economic catastrophe—for large numbers of displaced workers—the majority of them women—are the sole or primary supporters of their families. And many do not have—and find it very difficult to acquire—the skills needed to obtain other types of employment. For them, the availability or lack of availability of work in the apparel or textile industries represents the difference not between one job and another job, but the difference between making a living and living in poverty—between being a wage-earner or becoming a public charge.

So I hope that our negotiators dealing with the problems of tariffs on apparel and textiles keep the Egg Harbors and the Hammontons of America in mind. This is a human aspect of the problem—an aspect which cannot be measured by statistics.

The economic health of the towns and the cities of America is not expendable. That is why no cuts in tariffs should be made on any article of textiles or apparel. The existing regulation of imports is far too inadequate to supply proper safeguards to preserve jobs and work opportunities even though they are decidedly a step in the right direction. But very decidedly they must be supplemented by adequate tariffs. This is essential.

Mr. HILLIS. Mr. Speaker, I represent the Fifth Congressional District of Indiana, which includes most of Logansport, a small city of about 21,000 people located in the north-central part of the state. The H.W. Gossard Co. makers of girdles and brassieres, has a shop in Logansport. Not many years ago, this shop provided work for more than 200 people. Those 200 people and their dependents comprised a not insignificant portion of Logansport's consuming public. They spent their wages purchasing the products and services sold by the merchants of Logansport. They contributed a great deal to the economic well-being of the community.

The shop is still there today—still functioning. But it no longer employs 200 workers. By the latest count available to me, the work force in the plant is now down to 139. The massive flood of garment imports which has rolled over this country in the last several years has swept away the jobs of one-third of these workers, affecting not only the workers themselves and their families but the many others in Logansport who benefited directly and indirectly from their buying power—and, to a significant degree, the community as a whole.

But I have recently learned that Logansport is, in this regard, actually far more fortunate than several other communities. Not very long ago, this same firm had not just the one plant in Logansport, but four plants: two others in the State of Indiana and one up in the Upper Penninsula of Michigan. Taken together these 4 factories employed upward of 750 people.

Some time in 1975, the company was forced to terminate operations at its plant in Bicknell, Ind., where about 100 workers had been employed. At the end of 1976, the company's facilities at Ishpeming, Mich., which had provided employment for about 250 workers, was closed down. And just last month, a third of this company's factories shut down, this one located at Sullivan plant. Thus, in a relatively brief period, a firm which had employed some 750 workers has had to reduce its work force down to less than 140. Five-sixths of the jobs provided by this employer—over 600 in all—have disappeared. The products which the company produced are still in demand in this country, but that demand is now being met by products turned out not by the workers of Indiana and Michigan, but by workers and employers in places like Philippines and Haiti and Mexico, places where many workers are paid rates that are less than one-quarter or one-fifth of our legal minimum wage—let alone our average wage.

I said a moment ago that Logansport, because its plant is still in operation, is actually somewhat more fortunate than communities like Bicknell and Ishpeming and Sullivan, where shops have had to be shut down. Similarly, my own State of Indiana, while hard hit, is also in a sense more fortunate than a number of other states where the effects of the tide of garment imports verge on the disastrous. Florida has seen its apparel employment drop by 20 percent in only 3 years. Massachusetts and New Jersey have lost a quarter of their apparel jobs in a decade. In the same period, Pennsylvania has lost some 46,000 apparel jobs. Connecticut has lost some 29 percent of its apparel employment. In Illinois, almost 37 percent of the apparel jobs disappeared within 11 years. And fully 40 percent of the apparel jobs of New York—some 115,000— have gone down the drain.

These are very important figures, Mr. Chairman, for they indicate that the penetration of imports in the apparel trades in the American market has caused and is continuing to cause very severe disruptions in the economy of many communities and many States all over this country. I would hope that those who represent us in negotiating agreements with foreign countries, and those who administer the whole program are aware of the extent of this penetration and of the havoc it is causing.

There are still 139 workers left at the Gossard plant in Logansport. They and the remaining workers and producers in these affected industries look to our representatives at Geneva for some assurance of protection against the fate which has already befallen so many of their fellow Americans.

We look to them to except textiles and apparel in the course of the current negotiations for duty reductions. These industries cannot take it. Their workers cannot take it. The United States cannot take it and witness a further loss of employment, so much needed in our country in this day and age.

At least seventy congressmen and congresswomen spoke in the House and Senate to describe plant slowdowns and shutdowns in cities big and small across the country. Nevertheless, when the negotiators on the beautiful Swiss lake had completed their work in 1979, many tariffs on clothing and apparel were once again lowered. The plant at Logansport, Indiana, closed its doors in 1979.

B.
Unraveling A Union

**Knitgoods Local 190,
Philadelphia, Pa., August 21, 1973.**

The effect of imports on the American garment industry has varied. In 1977, for example, most dresses were still made in the United States, but one-third of the bras and girdles were not. Most skirts were still made here, but more than one-third of the coats and raincoats were imported.

Hardest hit was knitwear. In 1961, for every 100 sweaters made here in the USA only five were imported. By 1977, for every 100 sweaters made in the USA 109 were imported. *[See Chart Number 1.]*

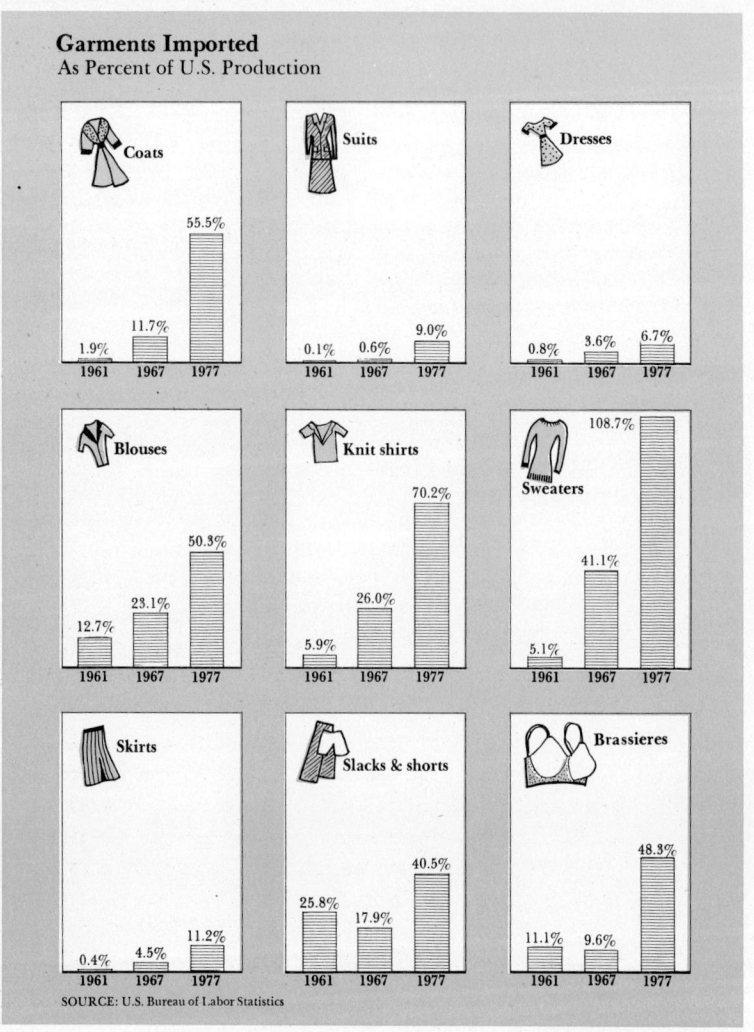

Garments Imported
As Percent of U.S. Production

Coats
- 1961: 1.9%
- 1967: 11.7%
- 1977: 55.5%

Suits
- 1961: 0.1%
- 1967: 0.6%
- 1977: 9.0%

Dresses
- 1961: 0.8%
- 1967: 3.6%
- 1977: 6.7%

Blouses
- 1961: 12.7%
- 1967: 23.1%
- 1977: 50.3%

Knit shirts
- 1961: 5.9%
- 1967: 26.0%
- 1977: 70.2%

Sweaters
- 1961: 5.1%
- 1967: 41.1%
- 1977: 108.7%

Skirts
- 1961: 0.4%
- 1967: 4.5%
- 1977: 11.2%

Slacks & shorts
- 1961: 25.8%
- 1967: 17.9%
- 1977: 40.5%

Brassieres
- 1961: 11.1%
- 1967: 9.6%
- 1977: 48.3%

SOURCE: U.S. Bureau of Labor Statistics

Chart Number 1

Challenged more than other unions, even other locals in the ILGWU, you who make knitwear have faced the critical challenge to your jobs due to the importation of the products you make. I am going to spend only a moment talking about it because I do not need to talk to knitgoods workers about the problems of imports.

You in local 190 were among the first in this country, in our union, to face this disaster. A number of years ago when this country was flooded with sweaters from Taiwan, Hong Kong, and other Far Eastern countries, even from some of the western democracies, we saw just that little cloud of sweaters and knitted shirts come over this industry. Perhaps some of us were not alert to what would happen if we did not act decisively to protect ourselves and thus protect our jobs. The auto workers were not worried about the first Volkswagons and Toyotas, either.

Today, many garment workers face this problem. Now it's not just sweaters, not just knitgoods, and not just Local 190 here in Philadelphia or Local 155, the knitgoods local in New York. Now it's many, many parts of our great International Union, sportswear, children's wear, nearly everything. Now many of our 450,000 members may be affected by the tremendous flood of ladies' apparel and knitted apparel from the low-wage countries overseas.

We do not seek to stop imports. What we do seek is to regulate them. We are willing to give people overseas opportunity for work and a fair opportunity to sell their goods here, but we cannot give them an unfair advantage at the expense of all of our own jobs, our families or our future. A strong labor movement here in the United States, with working men and women gainfully employed at a decent wage, benefits workers everywhere. When you are able to contribute to your families and to your communities, then, as strong trade unionists, you can turn your eyes to the rest of the world and help your brothers and sisters exploited in other countries.

The AFL-CIO, and particularly our own union, the ILGWU, traditionally has helped struggling union movements overseas. We have helped workers there to organize into unions so they also could negotiate and bargain collectively with their employers, so they also could raise their wages a few pennies an hour.

Believe it or not, twenty years ago, when ILG organizers first came to Puerto Rico, the workers there earned 6 cents, 8 cents and 13 cents an hour. Hard to believe! Today, after the ILGWU efforts in organizing those workers, they average $2.00, $2.20 and $2.30 per hour, and lest you think that is an extraordinarily low average, please compare it to their standard of living and to the other wages in that community. People who work in ILG shops are among the highest-paid industrial workers on the island of Puerto Rico. As a result, the workers there now have an opportunity to do more than survive. They have an opportunity to live.

While we ourselves do not organize in other countries, we have cooperated with workers in Holland, Germany, Italy, France and even in Japan. Our aid, our expertise, our advice, our support, is always given to workers the world over because we have one thing in common—the fight against exploitation. It is the fight for the right of working people to have something to say about their work, their working conditions and their share of the wealth they produce.

If American jobs are exported overseas, if there is an unregulated flow of imports, not only in apparel but also in radios, TVs, rubber goods, textiles, in almost everything we use, if American trade unions are weakened as a result, then workers overseas will be the losers because they live and work in communities where our help is needed. Workers in developing nations need the help of a strong American trade union movement to show them the example, to help them organize, to help them gain the courage and strength to stand up against their own governments. Too often such countries are controlled by the men who own the businesses, own the factories, own the money and the banks.

>At the end of 1973, when these remarks were made, Knitgoods Local 190 in Philadelphia had 6,471 members and Knitgoods Local 155 in New York had 16,473. By 1979, Local 190 had lost more than 1,200 members while Local 155 had

lost more than 7,000 members.

America's disastrous trade policies were making the following pattern: Knit one, purl two, drop all the stitches, and cast off American knitwear workers.

Meanwhile, garment workers in the low-wage countries overseas were not only no better off than before, they were often more exploited and more desperate.

four

Importing Mexico's Unemployment

Council for International Affairs, Harvard University, Cambridge, Mass., March 3, 1978.

The source of garment workers' travail lies in the push of the world's low-wage populations towards industrialization. International labor, business and government leaders of these countries meet to define, explore, debate and sometimes settle mutual problems. The Harvard Council holds workshops for international groups of business people on "the politics of international relations." This one was titled "Mexico, Balance and Prospects." Chaikin's assigned topic was "Mexico's Relations with the United States: A Labor Viewpoint."

Mexico is saddled with a government created by a pseudo-revolutionary party, characterized by trappings of democracy. The present government seems committed to oppression of the opposition. It is nearly an authoritarian state. It has not hesitated to use force and violence against labor, students and journalists, and we are concerned about this.

We have always known that a free trade union movement is a necessary bulwark of human rights and we do not see a free trade union movement in Mexico. Such a union movement acts as a catalyst toward a democratic ideal. It needs access to a free press and we are well aware of the removal of Julio Scherer, editor of your newspaper *Excelsior,* in 1976 during the Echeverria regime.

We know that the basis for revolution in Mexico was agrarian reform, but the inadequate redistribution of land has not satisfied the agrarian community. This, hand in hand with excessive unemployment and the inability of every Mexican government to ameliorate this problem, concerns us.

Mexico's governments to date have created circumstances where fewer and fewer people have more and more of the wealth, while more and more people have less and less. We in the United States labor movement are properly concerned about this.

There is a population explosion in Mexico. We cannot even get answers on the extent of the population growth. Can it be possible that the population increases at 3½ percent a year in spite of unemployment and the government's inability to solve the economic crisis? Millions are unemployed now; how many more will be unemployed in ten years? We see no population control plans, and we are concerned about this.

We see a country very poor, tied inexorably to the United States. Living with the United States is like getting into bed with an elephant, where even the swish of the tail can wreak havoc. We are aware of American imperialist influences that have sent American capital into Mexico. We are concerned about American industry's drive to use Mexican workers in labor-intensive industries.

We are aware of twin plant industries, one in Mexico manufacturing with disgracefully exploited labor, the other perhaps assembling or packing in the USA. We are aware of the quirks in the tariff laws that encourage these immoral marriages and that contribute to our own large unemployment. The profits, of course, are shared neither with the workers in Mexico nor with those here in the United States, and we are concerned about these laws.

We know there are thinkers and planners in Mexico who feel the solution to all their problems lies in labor-intensive work. There is no comparison between the costs of making things here or there. Poor Mexican garment workers average perhaps 59 cents an hour, while United States garment workers, who are at the low end of industrial wages here, earn more than

$4.00 an hour, plus many life-sustaining worker benefits. Thus, the drive toward "free trade," lowering tariffs and permitting low-cost goods to flood the United States has a deleterious effect on our workers, and we are concerned about this.

I might add that yours is not the only country who sees the U.S. marketplace as its salvation. There is a long line of countries as poor or poorer than yours waiting at our doors. We cannot absorb a flood tide of low-cost labor goods from all of you.

I should add, too, that an attempt at industrialization in other poor countries has had the disastrous effect of making their poor even poorer. Agriculturalization, not industrialization, may be the necessary first step.

Yet we take you at your word. We have accepted your rhetoric at face value, that we should share the values of political democracy. Then, all of a sudden, Mexico wants to become the leader of the Third World, but not to encourage democracy there. This has alarmed and disturbed us. Will you try to outdo the dictatorships? For though your per capita income is above that of the Third World, this position is not just an economic interest, it is a political grouping.

When authoritarian Argentina joins together with Mexico in this endeavor, we are distressed. At no time has it been more clear that Mexico was politically aligned with the non-democratic world than in siding against Zionism in the U.N. resolution of November 1975. Why should the AFL-CIO be concerned? Because Israel has had a free trade union movement since 1920. It can fairly be said that the Israeli government was both a democratic and a labor government. For Mexico to participate in that obnoxious vote is a source of concern.

At the ILO [International Labor Organization], Mexico's votes and interests have been disturbing, and we are concerned about this.

Mexico is exporting its unemployment to us. A river of poor humanity continuously flows across our border, fostered and encouraged by your government. We do not even know the enormity of the problem. From what we can guess, we believe eight to twelve million destitute Mexicans have flooded across in recent years, and we are concerned about this.

You could say these remarks have been critical, that we in labor have set ourselves up in an adversary position. Yet we do understand the problems and are not unsympathetic to the reasons that drive the people to come here. We ask ourselves, however, whether we can embark on a better policy of sharing. What will the present policy mean to the working class here? It is axiomatic that if United States workers are hurt, the more affluent groups here will not be far behind. Do we want to share the poverty?

We must therefore suggest reasonable solutions. Most leaders of the American trade union movement, if forced to think of Mexican workers, would be generous and forthcoming. But not generous about sharing all our work, lest we both collapse.

We in labor would say, "Organize your own free, democratic system. Do not mechanize your agriculture. Grow food for your own people and become self-sufficient in that regard. We are willing to give you grants-in-aid and more money in soft loans, and we should make payment of debts easier. Here we are a political democracy. We have a free trade union movement, a free press, and a large measure of freedom. We are not your enemy. We are no longer the stereotype of the United States back in 1935. But we will not support you if you react in opposition to us, or vote against us in the world arena, or if your political officers retire fat and wealthy, at the expense of the conditions of working people."

We know protective markets when we see them. We know protective devices when we meet them. We know free trade has not existed between us for generations. The United States is largely a free trade zone, but Mexico is closed. Trade relations have been a one-way street and the so-called free trade has been more illusory than real.

We want Mexico to grow stronger. We want Mexicans to be able to look forward to a better life. Yet we will not accept the brunt of policies that work in our disfavor. We must seek positive change.

We have yet to evolve a rational view as to how to live in this hemisphere.

QUESTION: I am impressed with your presentation and agree with much of what you said. I am a businessman from Mexico. You did not, however, differentiate between government and migrant workers. What about the pull factor?

CHAIKIN: Yes, there is a strong magnetic attraction towards the United States. We provide unparalleled economic opportunity as well as liberty. People all over the world are aware of these things and aspire to them, and they vote with their feet when they come. Between Mexico and the United States is the longest border, I believe, separating a poor nation from an affluent nation, so difficulties would not be unexpected. Perhaps the United States is to blame. Rather than herd people who come here into vehicles or let them swim across the Rio Grande, why can't our two governments agree that the United States can absorb X number of people each year along with guarantees for minimum wage and the rest? We are dealing with human beings. Europeans are no more civilized than the United States, though I envy them their love of wine, but they do have orderly processes of inviting what they call "guest workers" into home countries. Though the French leave something to be desired in how they treat Algerian workers, and other European countries in how they treat their "guests," it is a model to start from.

I would be the last to visit the sins of the government upon the heads of workers. I have nothing but sympathy for them. We have no humane policy and we should have. The labor movement would want to be helpful.

QUESTION: I am from the United States. You are distressed because of the increase of labor-intensive industry in Mexico. If Mexicans cannot come to work here, or are not permitted to export their products to us here, what can they do?

CHAIKIN: We are not opposed to their entering our markets. We just want to organize the entry. We are willing to share with them, but we cannot give every job away. We have our own Third World right here that cannot be retrained to work in steel, or computers, or other such available jobs. We must be able to

*Demonstration against imports,
November 16, 1972, Herald Square,
New York City.*

provide for them also. If we have orderly procedures, then other countries will get some share of our market and Americans can continue to have work as well.

> QUESTION: Undocumented workers—you have offered some suggestions on this problem. What do you believe we can do about those who are here now?

CHAIKIN: I agree with what President Carter has been saying, that those who have been here for five years or more should be allowed to stay and allowed citizenship. I have some problems with the idea of rounding up those who have been here only one or two years and shipping them back. That's vigilantism. We ought to be able as a country to accept, as business so often must, the big loss, because you know the problem will be handled better later. Let's accept what's done and find a better way for the future.

> QUESTION: The group here represents foreign investments, overseas investments. The AFL-CIO is opposed to this.

CHAIKIN: Not so willy-nilly. We are opposed to those activities that take the comparative advantage we had, the managerial know-how and sometimes the high technology and combine these with cheap labor to produce items overseas or across the border that are then brought back here to compete with United States labor.

We are not opposed to Ford going to Argentina to make cars for Argentinians. But when they go to Germany to build an Opel and bring it back here, or when they give up our industrial base here, like General Motors, to build GM trucks in Poland and turn over the factory keys to Poland, then we object. We will not get paid in money for this plant. Instead, we will get trucks to sell here. GM used Research and Development money that our people paid for to build there without a cent of it brought here for the people who worked for it and provided it.

What will the posture of our country, governed in a democratic spirit—and fewer than 24 countries are democratic today—when our muscles are cut because we do not have a manufacturing base? We will be a service-based economy and much poorer. Whom will you sell to in the United States if our markets are decimated because of greater and greater unemployment?

five

We Have So Much In Common, The United States And Britain

Chaikin travels out of the United States wearing two labor hats. As president of the ILGWU he articulates the special viewpoint of the American textile, clothing and apparel trades. As vice-president of the AFL-CIO he represents the interests of the broader organized labor movement in the United States. Reporting to his executive board he said:

Labor delegates in other countries have varying degrees of influence, Japan a moderate amount, and Korea a minimal amount. I believe that face-to-face discussions engender better understanding of America's problems, which in turn breeds a more cooperative attitude by foreign labor unions. If they accept our positions as reasonable, we can expect them to act as conduits to their governments who negotiate bilateral trade treaties with us. With a more forthcoming attitude, both parties can benefit as important quantative restraints and rules of the road are argued and settled.

Through my travels I try to advance the cause of free trade unionism around the world. My goals are to encourage the activities of labor unions, to bolster the U.S. economy, to assist those attempting to reorganize in the face of opposition and always to support working people here and abroad. In advanced democratic societies like England, Germany or Japan I want to maintain a relationship with their labor movements and argue our positions on issues like world trade.

**General Conference of the National Union
of Tailors and Garment Workers,
Scarborough, England, April 23, 1979.**

I will talk with you about things that trouble us in the United States. You will find that indeed we both have problems of great size. We have so much in common, the United States and Britain.

When you talk of wages, be assured that we suffer from the same disease and that disease is inadequacy. The average wages of the textile, apparel and clothing workers are hardly 50 percent of the average wages of all manufacturing employees in the United States. Yet our government persists in lumping all workers together in one homogenous Big Labor pool. In my conversations with the President of the United States and his counselors during a period when the voluntary 7 percent guidelines were being evolved, I made a point of saying over and over again that the most important element in any incomes policy, whether voluntary or not, must be fairness. It is just not fair to compare a 7 percent increase on an average wage of $9.00 or $10.00 an hour as obtains in the oil, steel and auto industries of our country, with a 7 percent increase on the average wage of textile, apparel and clothing workers of hardly $5.00 an hour. When you apply the same formula across the board you are not applying it to a national average. You are applying it to groups that have their own problems, their own standards, their own hurdles. If you apply one solid standard across the board, all you do is increase the gap between that first-tier group of organized labor in the United States, whom I call the "haves," and the second-tier group of workers within organized labor, whom I call the "have-nots."

Yes, we have the same problems that you have enunciated. I have read your agenda very carefully. I could take your chairman's eloquent report and use it at our own next conference without changing a word. Those policies, those problems and those suggestions are in the forefront of the minds and hearts of our own delegates. I could read the proposed agenda that you have before you and it could serve as one of our own. We battle daily to improve not only our wages but our working conditions—the setting of fair rates and changes in the workplace environment that we hope to make a little more humane and a little more acceptable.

We share so much, beginning with the fact that our country's greatness springs from your democratic history. The greatest single value we hold in common, regardless of our occasional differences, is our complete devotion to human rights and to free, democratic trade unionsim. I was delighted to hear references to your upcoming elections and to the interest that your delegates display in the success of the Labour Party candidates sometime next week. We, too, in the United States, in the textile, apparel and clothing industries, ask our members to become political citizens as well as industrial citizens, because we, too, find that it is only through the sovereign power that some of our problems must be approached. Unemployment and inflation, two demon traumas we share, are not problems that we can lick with collective bargaining alone.

I also note with special interest your espousal of the establishment of a national minimum wage law of not less than £60 [approximately $120], so that each worker can start on a base that would hardly make life sweet but would give him an opportunity to keep his head above the economic waters. We, too, petition our government to establish ever higher national minimum wages in our country. We are eager to improve them, not only because this approach offers some small measure of security to those without representation, but also because it sets a better standard for non-union competition from which our industry suffers.

You refer to the workers who lately have come to you from Third World countries, who are taken by the hand to the dark, dank and dingy places to work. They do not enjoy even the basic rudiments of economic protection, of economic equity, of justice and fairness. We, too, suffer from that because we, too, are a country ever renewing itself, ever welcoming to our shores the new immigrants who have come from the Hispanic countries, Southeast Asia and from Europe itself, even today.

We approach our government, not only to help maintain standards of decency and minimum standards of wages, but also to talk about a problem that has arisen in the last ten to fifteen years. We must determine whether or not we can evolve a rational system of international trade that does not beggar or destroy the job opportunities of workers in the western industrialized nations. We of the textile, apparel and clothing industries have been the first to suffer from the accelerated increase in imports from the unconscionably low-wage nations overseas. We have been very careful not to mount an attack on countries that are struggling to create a viable environment for all the workers, peasants and farmers, within their own borders. We are very aware of the need for us, who seem to have so much more, to care about the problems of the Third World and indeed to share with those people to some reasonable extent, so that they be given an opportunity through their own sweat, ability and conscientious attention to duty, to move toward lives of dignity and self-respect. But what would it avail them if, in doing that, a million jobs in the United Kingdom were washed overseas? How would it help them if the sinews and the strength of industrial America were sapped because we turned our heads from what has been happening through the enormous imports of textiles and apparel?

Do we not also share your concern with the rush of Red China to join the twentieth century, then perhaps, to move beyond that to the twenty-first century? I mean the rush of Red China to seek the fruits of our industrialization by making agreements with your country's manufacturers and ours to buy capital-intensive machinery.

What would come to our shores to pay for this costly machinery? What is Red China capable of producing with a minimum of capital investment but with a maximum of low-paid workers—hundreds of millions of workers within her borders? Will it be the traditional route of other underdeveloped countries who go into the manufacture of textile, apparel and clothing? We know it can be done quickly and simply without a great deal of technological innovation.

We have argued this with our government, just as we have discussed it with you. We have sent observers and delegates to the renegotiation of the Multifiber Arrangements. Over the past years we have been engaging daily in the negotiation of bilateral agreements with the great textile and clothing exporters around the world. We have joined with you in moving forward our common concern of sharing with Third World countries our rich domestic markets. But now we say to our government that there has been sufficient importing and the time has come to hold onto remaining work opportunities. They are needed desperately not only in our country but in your country as well.

We have met with some small measure of success only because we act as political citizens. Only when citizens take political responsibilities seriously will their pleas, petitions and entreaties be met with some measure of understanding and appreciation in the corridors of government power.

We have so much in common. I said at the outset that we shared many of the same problems, but we in the United States are not so large and we are not so smart, nor are we so successful that we cannot learn from you. I hope and expect as a result of your deliberations to take home many ideas for possible solutions.

six

The Labor Summit

**Labor Union Leaders Conference,
Tokyo, Japan, June 22, 1979.**

The Labor Union Leaders Conference, which came to be known as the Labor Summit, assembled in Tokyo a few days before the Tokyo Summit, where President Carter met with the six other heads of state from the major industrialized democratic countries.

This Labor Summit, third and largest of its kind, brought together thirty-three top officials from unions in the same seven countries participating in the political summit: USA, Britain, Canada, Germany, France, Italy and Japan. Five international labor groups were also represented: International Confederation of Free Trade Unions (ICFTU), its Asian Regional Organization (ARO) that speaks for the less developed countries of Asia, European Trade Union Congress (ETUC), World Confederation of Labor (WCL), and the Trade Union Advisory Committee (TUAC).

The Labor Summit gave these always separated and sometimes antagonistic union leaders the rare opportunity to talk informally with each other about the impact of various national policies upon the workers they each represent and, additionally, to have, in the words of a press release, "the voice of workers in various nations reflected in the Summit."

Chaikin represented the AFL-CIO as he had at the first Labor Summit, held in London in 1977. In 1978, in Bonn, Germany, Lane Kirkland (now president of the AFL-CIO) spoke for the organization. Advising them was Irving Brown, AFL-CIO representative to Europe.

The conference was widely covered by Japanese papers, radio, and TV and by broadcasts throughout Europe and Southeast Asia. Chaikin was interviewed often. The following transcript combines two separate press conferences from leading newspapers, *Mainichi* and *Yomiuri* and covers issues not included in the official statement to Prime Minister Masayoshi Ohira, which follows the transcript.

REPORTER: What is the purpose and what do you expect of this Labor Summit in Tokyo?

CHAIKIN: First of all, we hope to be able to acquire insights into our common problems by gathering together in a hall to share our experiences. Secondly, because nations share common problems in different forms, comparisons will lead to objective evaluations of the problems themselves. Thirdly, as we gain more practice in thinking about our common problems, we may discover common solutions.

Industrially-advanced nations face similar problems. Inflation, unemployment, energy and so on are now weighing heavily on Americans, and I want workers to take them up as problems common to many nations, not ours alone. I also want workers to consider an economic order for securing equality among nations, because such equality is a necessary measure to cope with the situation.

REPORTER: What views do you have about the problems of full employment and economic growth, which have been consistently demanded by labor?

CHAIKIN: In the United States, we in the labor movement are most strongly opposed to carrying out anti-inflation measures by financial means—the so-called deflationary policy—because this will lower social welfare and hurt the interest of workers.

The government must not try to stop inflation by causing unemployment. Moreover, I believe that a reasonable scale of economic growth to take care of a growing population will not necessarily cause inflation. Oil and other energy problems have become the focal points in connection with economic growth, and there are very great differences among the seven participant nations. Japan and West Germany rely on imports. Britain is hastening self-sufficiency with her new oil fields. The United States has many kinds of resources, yet we import in large quantities. Therefore, the situations in the various nations are different. For this reason, much discussion will be necessary.

We will probably not seek a strong confrontation with OPEC. OPEC cannot survive without the advanced nations of the West, which includes Japan. It is necessary to establish cooperation.

> REPORTER: What do you think about the results of the two Labor Summit Conferences in the past, held in London and Bonn?

CHAIKIN: While the Advanced Nations Conference, the political summit, started four years ago in 1975, our Labor Summit began only two years ago. Each nation's own policies alone are insufficient in this age of interdependence. Especially in regard to economic problems, it can be said that the time has ripened for workers to hold international talks.

The past two conferences have not greatly affected the thinking of the government leaders who participated in the Summits. For the most part, unemployment has increased and inflation is worsening; workers generally are disappointed and distressed. However, as cooperative actions among industrial democracies increase, as they must, the participation of workers in labor summits will become more meaningful.

> REPORTER: There are many cases where the labor unions of various nations have to compete with each other. Is it not difficult for representatives of labor unions coming from various nations to produce a joint proposal at the Labor Summit?

CHAIKIN: Yes, there is friction, but first, how many similarities are there between the International Ladies' Garment Workers' Union and the National Federation of Textile Industry Workers Union [Zensen] in Japan? We have a fine relationship with Tadanobu Usami, [now president of Domei, the Japanese counterpart to the AFL-CIO] and we find we are beginning to be more alike than perhaps was imagined a short while ago. There are common problems, such as being undercut by low-wage, almost no-wage countries like Korea and Taiwan, which has only recently begun to happen to you in Japan.

There are differences, however. At the London Summit, Mr. Shioji of Domei presented his government's view and as a result, found himself in disagreement with us, namely that Japan limit its automobile exports. Mr. Shioji absolutely

Japanese Textile Unions Seek Import Restraints

by Tsukasa Furukawa

TOKYO (Cable FNS)—Japan's textile labor unions, which until several years ago, rapped Americans for restricting Japanese imports, are now spearheading the move in this country for import restraints.

Zensen, Japan's national Federation of Textile-Apparel Workers Unions, has passed a resolution calling on the Japanese government to conclude, as early as possible, bilateral agreements under the Multi-Fiber Agreement (MFA), covering cotton yarn, cotton fabrics and other specific items.

The prime candidates for bilaterals at this point are said to be South Korea and Taiwan, with the People's Republic of China hovering in the future as another bilateral prospect.

The resolution, adopted at Zensen's annual convention in Nagoya, did not mention any countries. But it called for an eventual conclusion of comprehensive bilateral agreements with exporter countries on all textile products.

Until such bilateral agreements are concluded, effective administrative guidance should be exercised to establish order in the import market, the resolution said.

A Zensen spokesman told FNS that the resolution has been sent to the Ministry of International Trade and Industry (MITI) and various political parties in this country.

Zensen said imports of textile products to Japan last year shot up 56.7 percent to $2,530 million more than the previous year. Imports during the first seven months of this year soared to $2,050 million, the spokesman said.

"If imports continue at this high level, it will nullify all the efforts and sacrifices the Japanese textile industry has made in the protracted slump," Zensen said.

"The United States and European Economic Community are protecting the jobs of workers of their textile industries through bilateral agreements based on the Multi-Fiber Agreement (MFA)," the spokesman said. "It is only Japan which, among the industrial nations, has its textile-

objected to this proposal. Heinz Vetter, the West German representative, strongly objected to our suggestion that Germany and the U.S. reflate their economies to provide the engine for economic recovery.

REPORTER: How do you view the export of Japanese products to the United States?

CHAIKIN: To be sure, Japanese products have given rise to difficulties in the U.S. economy. On the other hand, they have brought about useful results, too. The advance of Japanese products has caused managers and capitalists in the U.S, to feel it absolutely necessary to make their business more competitive, to increase productivity and to improve the quality of their products.

In the United States there is a new way of thinking that favors "fair trade" rather than "free trade." This might take the form of restrictions that would permit a share of the growing American market to others, but leave a more equitable share for Americans.

May I say that there are many points that I do not understand about the Japanese economy.

REPORTER: Concretely, what points of the Japanese economy are hard to understand?

apparel market completely open to imports and which looks on with folded arms at the destruction of its own industry."

Zensen's call for import quotas reflected the growing sentiment in industry circles here demanding some steps to restrict imports.

It followed reports that the Japan Textile Federation was asking the government here to invoke provisions of GATT and MFA to protect the industry from rising imports.

Earlier this month, the Japan Export Clothing Manufacturers Association (JECMA) approved the position for an extension of MFA which was to expire at the end of this year.

Reprinted by permission of The Daily News Record, *Fairchild Publications, Inc., September 24, 1979.*

CHAIKIN: For example, I hear that Japanese TVs are sold more cheaply in the United States than in Japan because of the complicated domestic distribution system in Japan. I cannot understand why the distribution system is so complex and why there are so many middlemen.

Moreover, it is hard to understand why the Japanese market is not opened up to a fair level of imports.

Also, why does the Japanese housing situation remain so bad, although the economic power of Japan has increased so much?

OFFICIAL STATEMENT AT THE "LABOR SUMMIT," TOKYO, JAPAN, JUNE 22, 1979.

> The thirty-three delegates to the Labor Summit chose five speakers to sum up their consensus views for Japanese Prime Minister Ohira. The Prime Minister, host for the political summit, had agreed to present the labor resolutions to the Heads of State so that their anxieties might be reflected at the Tokyo Summit.
>
> Seije Amaike, President of Domei, the Japanese Federation of Labor, gave a general analysis of economic issues, noting that the labor group was encouraged by the concerted action of the industrialized countries which, since the 1978 Summit, had resulted in moving the world economy at least partially out of the OPEC-induced 1974-75 recession. He said the effort was not sufficient, however, to produce the full employment of true recovery and he predicted a further downtrend.
>
> Heinz Vetter, President of the DGB, Germany's major labor organization, reported on the question of employment and economic growth. He emphasized the labor group's unanimous resolution: Full employment should be the immediate goal of all economic policy, to be achieved through economic growth. He cautioned against vigorous deflationary measures that could only aggravate recession and cause more unemployment. He observed that both unemployment and inflation had grown worse during the last year and social disintegration, like that of the 1930s, could result, a danger certain to be exacerbated by any attempt at dismantling existing social safeguards.
>
> Dr. P.P. Narayanan and Otto Kersten, President and General Secretary of the International Confederation of Free

Union Leaders at Labor Summit, Tokyo, Japan, June 22, 1979. Chaikin is third from left.

Trade Unions, ICFTU, reported the Labor Summit's resolve to cooperate in solving North-South problems, particularly as they relate to Third World countries.

Chaikin's official statement, slightly condensed here, was limited to the twin issues of the OPEC oil monopoly and the need for the "harmonization" of international labor standards, a term used to mean the raising of low pay rates and benefits in all countries so that wages become more nearly equal worldwide.

Mr. Prime Minister:

I wish to confine my remarks to two essential points of the memorandum that we are presenting to the Heads of State meeting here in Tokyo. These two crucial sectors are energy and international labor standards.

1. It is quite clear that the major consumers of oil are faced with a common problem that can be met only with coordinated planning and controls to negotiate with the major oil-producing countries in OPEC.

We are seeking collective negotiations that would embrace not only the question of price but also the problem of the distribution and redistribution of supplies. We are not seeking adversary confrontation, but neither should we submit meekly to arbitrary demands.

Such a cooperative approach does not diminish the need for continuing energy conservation policies. Nor should exploration and long-range efforts to secure alternate sources of energy be decreased. Rather, such programs should be greatly increased with larger amounts of capital made available for them.

Price and taxation policies aimed at increasing the profits of the oil companies, in the hope that they will invest more in exploration and research to increase the available supplies, have not achieved the desired results. Only a small fraction of these profits is used for such purposes while most of their "windfall" profits are diverted by the oil companies to take over firms in other economic sectors. Therefore, governments themselves must accept much greater direct responsibility in investment policies and planned development of new sources of energy.

More efficient use of energy will not be achieved through high prices. Energy conservation must be mandatory. Stringent standards must be set to this effect by legislation and regulation. Large-scale rehabilitation of public transport and the promotion of energy-saving standards in the housing sector are particularly important. In addition, throughout the manufacturing sector there are many specific ways to shift from energy-intensive to more energy-saving production processes. Here again, major governmental initiatives are needed.

Concerted action is required in all these areas of

energy policy. Energy must be a major priority since it is essential to maintain and expand employment. Moreover, the industrial nations must first put their own houses in order. Unless they do, they cannot help the developing nations.

It is therefore proposed that the Heads of State meeting in Tokyo consider the necessity to recommend that a conference of the industrialized consumer nations be called to arrive at a common approach and create an organization to negotiate with the petroleum-producing nations. This should not exclude eventually including the oil-consuming nations of the developing world.

2. International harmonization of labor standards must be intensified. ILO [International Labor Organization] conventions and recommendations must be followed to promote better living standards, employment, and growth in both developed and developing countries.

Considerable differences in wage rates and working conditions exist among countries at comparable levels of economic development and strength. These wide differences affect all aspects of cooperation and joint action among our seven countries. They severely distort international trade and the international monetary system. Unless energetic steps are immediately taken to remove these inequalities, which have no economic justification, many beneficial effects of other cooperative ventures could be jeopardized.

Sustained efforts should therefore be made to harmonize working hours, the standards of social security, health and safety, working environment, and trade union rights throughout the industrialized world. In addition, specific measures aimed at improving the living and labor standards in the developing countries should be encouraged as an integral part of development assistance in all its forms.

Thank you, Mr. Prime Minister.

seven

Best Of A Bad Bargain

Trade Subcommittee of the Senate Committee on Finance, Washington, D.C., July 19, 1979.

By mid-1979, the ILGWU's fight to save the jobs of America's garment workers was going forward on several fronts. Chaikin's travels abroad were building institutional contacts that were helping to make other countries aware of the consequences of current international trade agreements. At home, the work of lobbying Congress had intensified as the dates approached when Congress was to vote on the trading arrangements that had finally been hammered out.

The ILGWU lobbies with expert testimony. Lazare Teper, Ph.D., Johns Hopkins, economist and the director of research, is generally regarded as one of the country's leading authorities on international trade. As the "eyes, ears and legs" of president Chaikin, he is often in Asia or Europe as an advisor to American governmental teams negotiating trade agreements.

Chaikin and Teper made many appearances together before many congressional committees and subcommittees. Meeting here almost four years to the day after the 1975 hearing in Chapter 3 is the Trade Subcommittee chaired by Daniel Patrick Moynihan (D-NY). Under discussion is another trade "liberalization," meaning "tariff cut," pact. But it is not a minor bill. This one concerns the MTN, the Multilateral Trade Negotiations that have taken years to write and that will govern world-wide trade for many years to come.

The MTN bill had just been approved overwhelmingly by the House of Representatives, 395 to 7. Greatly alarmed, but many months too late to take part in the horse-trading, a few New York garment manufacturers had charged in the press that these tariff cuts would be calamitous for the garment industry in New York. They requested a Senate hearing in advance of the Senate vote on the same bill, to come up in only four days, ten days after the House landslide vote.

The manufacturers' testimony, given just before Chaikin's, roundly condemned the proposed bill, and a No vote by the Senate was urged.

Chaikin's testimony makes three points: (1) The actual amounts of tariff cuts are very small for garments hurt by imports. The cuts are somewhat larger for garments not so hurt by imports. (2) Tariffs alone cannot control low-wage imports. The real hope for import relief lies with quotas carefully tied to the growth of the American market. (3) While the trade package is the best of a bad bargain for the garment industry, it gives Congress and the country four or five years to develop a rational trade policy.

CHAIKIN: Mr. Chairman, Senator Moynihan. I want to thank you for the opportunity that you have given to me and my colleagues to spend a few moments with the committee. I know you will forgive me if I articulate our concerns in a fairly informal manner.

Back in 1961 when you and Deputy Assistant Secretary of State W. Michael Blumenthal and Assistant Secretary of Commerce Hickman Price, attempted to represent the best interests of those of us who were concerned with the wide-ranging problems of the textile, cotton, and apparel industries, our union became concerned with what we then discerned as a small cloud no larger than a man's hand. That small cloud was the fact that, although we had a fairly thriving domestic ladies' and children's apparel industry, we could see some years down the road when there would be significant inroads into our domestic market by countries that were attempting to come onstream and take their place in the industrial life of the world community.

Back in 1961, for every hundred pieces of ladies' and children's apparel made in the United States, four pieces were made overseas and sold here. We welcomed the importing of these items because generally they came as high-quality goods—silks from Italy, haute couture designs from France, woolens from Great Britain.

Our union, which then as now represents a broad-based membership in thirty-eight states plus Puerto Rico and Canada, was anxious that the domestic industry become more creative, more competitive with the best in the world. We thought that the imports from Paris, Rome and London, with the attendant publicity and hoopla about their esoteric, exclusive designs, would challenge our domestic American designers.

Indeed, the imports then served that purpose. Today, without qualification we can say that the heart and soul of innovative design, creative fashion design, lies on Fashion Avenue, New York's Seventh Avenue in the United States of America.

During this intervening period other things happened. One was that less-developed nations discovered that with a minimum investment, with very simple machinery, with American managerial know-how that was easily found and with software easily transported, they could set up competing garment production almost anywhere in the world. And they did.

As a result, from four pieces of apparel coming in from overseas for every one hundred pieces made in the U.S. in 1961, we now come to 1978, this past year, when we find that more than fifty pieces of ladies' and children's wear come in from overseas for every one hundred pieces made in this country.

Now this is import penetration of an extraordinary degree, and it has occurred in spite of the fact that over the last sixteen or seventeen years our union voice, powerful as it may have been in certain limited areas of political life in our own communities, has been a voice crying in the wilderness here in the halls of Congress.

Our domestic market has been penetrated to an alarming extent. As far as the textile, apparel and clothing industries are concerned, many billions of dollars have been lost, not only because of this import penetration, but also because, as a result, we were not able to add to the employment rolls what might naturally have been expected from the growth of the United States population over the last two decades.

When we talk of ladies' and children's garment workers, we mean some 350,000 ILGers. I want to remind you that just ten years ago our union had 460,000 members. By analyzing the number and kind of clothes that are imported, Dr. Teper has estimated that 178,000 more people would be working in the United States today to produce the clothes now imported.

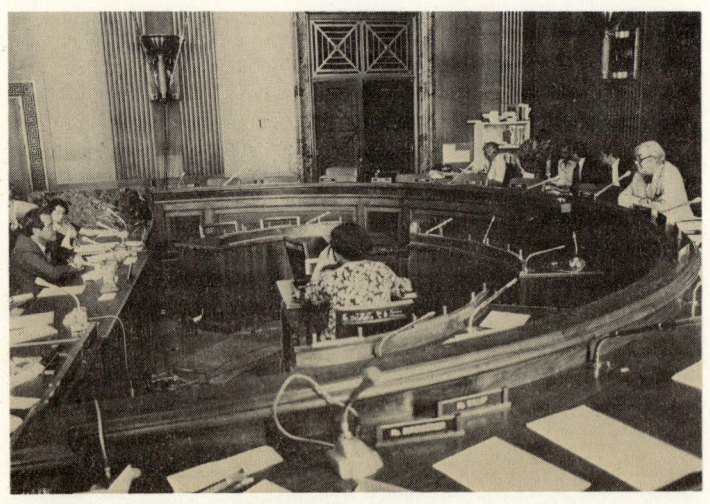

ILGWU pres. Sol C. Chaikin (left), with vice-president Evelyn Dubrow, testifying in support of trade legislation before Senate hearing in Washington, chaired by New York Senator Daniel Patrick Moynihan (right).

There is no question about our credentials in this matter, Senator Moynihan. We have consistently, persistently and forcefully represented what we believe to be the best interests of workers of this country and indeed of our industry. In truth, we have always been somewhat concerned over the fact that the owners and managers of this industry—strong though they may have been, profitable though they are on occasion and full of voice as they have demonstrated here earlier this morning— have been quiet in the past. Their voices were quiet, their presence was nowhere to be found. Interest in this matter, although overriding to us, seemed to be of minimal importance to them.

I recall very well two and a half years or so ago when many of the employers from New York City went down to Washington at the invitation of this union to attend our leadership and legislative conference. One of the most important items on our agenda was imports. We asked them to participate with us as observers of our lobbying for greater fairness about trade. After that conference, I exhorted the employers to form an organization to afford them an independent voice, an independent posture.

I said to them that I thought the way Congress is constituted, the influence of the employers and manufacturers and men of wealth might be greater in many ways than the influence of organizations of workers. The formation of the employers' group was, I think, primarily at the urging of the International Ladies' Garment Workers' Union.

We are happy to have them giving voice to their own concerns; that is the way it should be. Obviously, the employers speak to their own self-interests, as they must, but I would hope that they will develop a broader-gauged concern for all the industry in this country, because self-interest, admirable though it may be, will occasionally be harmful if it is so ego-centered as to ignore wider values and problems.

We in the labor movement have recognized early on the fact that our only salvation for keeping a share of this domestic market for the hundreds of thousands of workers we represent is quantitative restraint: in short, quotas. We have directed all of our energy, all of our effort, in that direction.

When the Carter administration came into office, we met with the President and with his special trade representative, Robert Strauss, together with other representatives of other parts of the textile, apparel and clothing industries. We, of course, have a long and abiding and cooperative relationship with our brother and sister union, the Amalgamated Clothing and Textile Workers, the people who make men's clothing as well as textiles. It is natural for the two unions to cooperate.

But when we reached out to a broader coalition, we were occasionally ill at ease. Although we had an important community of interest with certain groups, we were, aside from this issue, at loggerheads at other times and other places.

I am referring to the largely non-union textile industry. When the textile mill owner sees an item of ladies' apparel coming into this country, his only thought is that it is a piece of fabric that he should have woven in his own mill. When we see that same item come in, we say, "That is an hour's worth of labor that should have been given to and paid to a U.S. garment worker."

But workers and employers have a community of interest on the question of imports, so we got together with them and

At the White House discussing the impact of imports on textiles and apparel: (l. to r.) Jack Sheinkman, secretary-treasurer Amalgamated Clothing and Textile Workers Union; Murray Finley, president ACTWU; Vice-President Walter Mondale behind Finley; Sol Chick Chaikin, president ILGWU; Dr. Lazare Teper, ILGWU director of research; Robert Strauss, Special Assistant to the President; President Jimmy Carter; George Meany president AFL-CIO. April 13, 1977.

with other representatives of the dyers, the spinners, the woolgrowers, cottongrowers—an entire range of ad hoc interests. Together, we zeroed in on the broad general problems in textile, apparel and clothing.

Two and one-half years ago, when the Carter administration came into office, we approached them jointly and told them of our troubles: that in spite of eighteen bilateral agreements with eighteen separate countries, in spite of attempts at quotas, a greater share of the domestic market was being eaten away by imports from unconscionably low-wage areas overseas.

Let me add here that both the Amalgamated Clothing Workers and we in the ILGWU have always been concerned about the developing nations and about the workers in those countries who are striving for an opportunity to lift themselves out of unspeakable and indescribable poverty. It was never our intention to build high tariff walls or to have the kind of quantitative restraints—quotas—that would keep their products altogether out of this country.

But by the same token, we could not be so generous as to invite those products in to such an extent that our employers go out of business themselves. So always we were concerned to strike a reasonable balance between maintaining work opportunities for the workers we represent and for workers overseas.

And we always thought that what the shares should be was a matter of negotiation, of accommodation, of discussion and argument, of give and take until, finally, a decision would be reached.

We said to this new administration that, in the past, as we negotiated these things, we discovered that they were not working out in the way we had hoped, that the inroads being made were too wide and too deep, that the denial of work opportunities to American workers was now becoming more than a passing interest. Denial of work was becoming a major item on the agenda, not only of textile workers, but of much of American industry across the board, as one by one, factories of all varieties closed here in the United States.

We began to pressure the President's special representative, Bob Strauss, and anybody else to whom we could reach out, including yourself, Senator Moynihan, to have an awareness of

Chaikin (left) with Dr. Lazare Teper, ILGWU director of research, at Senate hearing, July 19, 1979.

including yourself, Senator Moynihan, to have an awareness of this problem. We want negotiation of the new bilateral agreements as part of a tougher overall stance so that the well-known generosity of Americans might be tempered somewhat, so that the rate of the annual increase in established quotas would more nearly reflect the annual increase in domestic demand.

Domestic demand has increased only about 2 percent a

year over any reasonable prior period, but imports under the terms of the MFA have been permitted to burgeon by 6 percent or more per year, compounded. But for the last two years, during all the horsetrading of the Multilateral Trade Negotiations and the bilateral trade agreements and the quotas, we received no help at all from the employers in New York City who are here represented today. An invitation had been extended to them to participate in regular meetings, but they missed the boat. We forgive them their inaction as we hope they occasionally forgive us our transgressions.

The ILGWU and the garment manufacturers are not always antagonists. We are not here today in an adversary posture. But they come now to cast doubt on the past year and a half. Having missed the opportunity to participate, they are confused about the importance of the tariff cuts being proposed. The tariff cuts they so vehemently object to are not so critical as they might think.

Whether you reduce the tariffs by 5 percent more or 5 percent less has little or no relationship to the cost of the garment if it is made in a southeast Asian country. China, for example, is sending apparel into this country subject to tariffs that are far above those that apply to most exporting countries. These higher tariffs did not check their exports. This trade bill will not help one bit to stop the Chinese flood.

The difference between the wage costs in Red China, Taiwan, Hong Kong and South Korea today and the wage costs paid in New York City is enormous. Add to that the American employers' overhead costs, their taxes, the general cost of doing business, plus the costs of OSHA [Occupational Safety and Health Act], the requirements of our environmental laws, or the worker benefits applied over and above the direct wages. Our costs are not comparable to theirs, so how much difference will a few cents' reduction in tariffs make?

If it costs $30.00 here to make a dress at Jerry Silverman's company, that same dress could cost $1.50 to $2.50 in Hong Kong, and no amount of tariff applied to the true value of that garment as it comes out of the Hong Kong factory can make up for this great divergence in cost.

What I am trying to say, simply, Senator Moynihan, is that I welcome the voices of these employers. I welcome their newfound interest. I welcome their newfound concern, but I think it was misapplied in this particular circumstance.

Of course, we in the ILG would have preferred no tariff reduction. In our judgment, with Dr. Teper as an advisor, involved as he is in an unofficial way with the negotiations, we tell you this trade bill, this Multilateral Trade Negotiations [MTN], is the best of a bad deal. Yet, we support it and we say that these employers ought to support it as well. They should not be discouraged.

The problem that they see can be ameliorated in large part not only by quotas tied to our growth, but also by the application of the agreement that was reached between the President of the United States, the special trade representative and our ad hoc group representing textile, apparel and clothing interests. You were present at the White House meeting.

We put great stock in that agreement. We believe that the administration will carry out not only its words but its spirit as well.

We know that the quotas are set in the bilaterals, those agreements made with specific countries. We know that Robert Strauss, the special trade representative, and his department, particularly Ambassador Michael B. Smith, are negotiating to hold the feet of the exporters in Korea, Hong Kong and other places to the fire.

We know that pressures put on Strauss have been greater in the past six months than at any time in the past. We also know that the process by which these tariffs have been reduced has been long argued. The process has been difficult and probably unsatisfactory to every one of us involved. Our first position, from which we moved only at the last moment, was that the tariff cuts for textiles and apparel be taken off the table, not discussed. We knew, however, even though we took that extreme position, that we could not end up in that position because the administration had insisted that cuts had to be made.

I might add, parenthetically, that these employers whom

you heard earlier today, so steadfastly unwilling to bend, have never agreed to give to the negotiators of the ILGWU their first and major demands at the bargaining table. They must learn to use these self-same bargaining skills in international negotiating.

Senator Ernest F. Hollings (D-SC) introduced a bill opposing tariff cuts. You supported it and other senators voted for it, but it could not come to reality. At that point we entered into conversation with Bob Strauss, the President's special trade representative, to suggest that if the U.S. government had to participate in tariff-cutting procedures, it might pay practical attention to reducing tariffs in those areas that were not already dangerously hurt by imports. And this they did.

I want to say clearly and unequivocally that our union supports the MTN, Multilateral Trade Negotiations. But I also want to repeat simply and clearly that I believe it is the best of a bad bargain. We would all have been much happier if there were no tariff reductions.

I think the most important thing about the MTN is that it has been completed. The tariff cuts will take place over the next decade. As a union officer, I would hope that we have gained four or five years during which the American community, the U.S. Congress, the Senate, the executive, plus the industries in the USA can take a good, hard look at the entire trade problem and begin to evolve the policies that will result in a rational trade policy for all segments of our industrial society and for all members of our U.S. community.

> MOYNIHAN: I would like to introduce into the record at this point a summary of the administration's textile program which was agreed to February 15, 1979, in the White House, and which you helped negotiate. It follows the President's statement of November 11, 1978, in which you were also involved.
>
> I think that what you say is profoundly important. We have the MTN, the Multilateral Trade Negotiations. That means we have four or five years in which American industry can get itself together on this whole question of how we are going to compete in the world. This is particularly true for the apparel industry. There is no change of tariffs for two and one-half years ahead of us, no changes of any kind. The reductions come in very

slowly later.

We have forgotten the Smoot-Hawley tariff in the 1930s with the world crashing down, the depression that fed the flames of fascism in Europe. We must remember that tariff walls will not solve world problems.

What you have said is that quantitative restraint, quotas, must be related to the actual increase in domestic demand, not some hypothetical increase like 6 percent. Two percent sounds right.

I think this is reality and I think you have dealt with reality. In this particular reality, if I am not mistaken, you now have seventeen years. Is that not right, sir? Seventeen years of this negotiation. It did not start yesterday. Your economist, Dr. Teper, was a young man, and he is reaching vigorous middle age on these matters.

As you know, one of the reasons this hearing is being held is that we are not just adopting a new agreement in the Tokyo Round, which has as its object our getting access to markets that have been closed to us. With New York City as the fashion capital of the world, we could export if we could get through the myriad barriers that have been put up against us. This MTN is such a breakthrough.

I do not have to tell those of you who have been in this battle from the first that the entire bias of the U.S. government was against you when you went in. They said you were wrong, that there was something offensive about the whole idea of quotas, and that this was just fending against the Holy Spirit, as Cordell Hull put it.

You have brought the government around, kicking and screaming with great institutional resistance. You have succeeded so well that I do not think there would be any responsible person around right now who would not agree that we have to have quantitative restrictions.

We are also in the process of reorganizing the machinery of the United States government for dealing with trade policy. The President has promised us this and we are waiting for the new arrangements, any day now. We want to build into the machinery of the government a vigilant attention to the issues that you have raised.

For all these years the ILGWU has really worked at enforcement of trade agreements and now it has to be something the U.S. government wants to do, not is just willing to do if it has no other choice forced upon it. The government has to see enforcement as the legitimate right of U.S. business.

I see you nodding on the whole question of implementation being essential. We in government are just getting to that point, and we have two tools. One is the agreement with the administration that you yourself negotiated based on the principle of quantitative restrictions whose growth rate is to be tuned to the growth of the market. The second is a new set of arrangements within the United States government that will implement this agreement and do so out of the conviction that it is a good agreement, not simply a compromise, not an embarrassment imposed upon us.

We welcome the manufacturers. They are relatively newly organized. We welcome them as future partners.

I see Mr. Chaikin nodding vigorously. It would be very uncharacteristic of him if he did not.

>Four days after this hearing, the Senate followed the House and overwhelmingly approved the historic Trade Act of 1979, 90 to 4. President Carter signed the bill July 27, 1979, at a White House ceremony attended by Chaikin.

eight

Coping With A Changed World

Committee for Economic Development (CED),
San Francisco, California, May 17, 1979, and the
Council of Foreign Relations (CFR),
New York, New York, October 17, 1979.

On April 12, 1979, the key trading nations of the world completed five years of discussions in Geneva, held under the auspices of the international organization known as GATT, the General Agreement on Tariff and Trade. These negotiations are referred to as the Tokyo Round (the 1973 decision to conduct them was reached in Tokyo), or as the Multilateral Trade Negotiations (MTN).

Once negotiations were completed, each of the 99 participating nations had to approve the decisions officially. As of this writing, some key countries have done so. The bill ratifying these agreements was adopted in the United States on July 27, 1979, and is known as the Trade Act of 1979.

Issues in the MTN which affect labor in international trade matters were touched upon by Chaikin in a speech before the trustees of the CED when congressional passage of the Trade Act was expected. Some of these remarks were also presented during a seminar sponsored by the CFR.

The CED is an organization whose corporate members for the most part represent U.S. financial and industrial interests and whose individual members are among the chief executive officers of U.S. companies. The Council on Foreign Relations is an organization of individuals interested in U.S. foreign policy.

U.S. Garment Factory
Justice *Photo,*
Jerry Soalt

The Multilateral Trade Negotiations will reduce tariffs throughout the world over an eight-year period. According to President Carter, the most important achievement of the Tokyo Round is a series of codes of conduct regulating nontariff barriers to trade. Codes on subsidies, countervailing duties and anti-dumping will attempt to limit trade distortions arising from such practices and provide ways to challenge and counteract them when they cause material injury or breach agreed rules. Only time will tell how well they will work.

The countries of the world are now so tied together economically that national policies have global consequences. All of our own efforts at trade negotiations have been directed in the name of "free trade," a slogan from the 1930s that masks this radically changed nature of the world. Other countries are not free trading zones for our goods, yet they all come knocking at our doors demanding instant entry, and we try to oblige. As a direct result, serious damage is being done to the industrial fabric of our country. Until recently there has been inadequate representation of another point of view. I want to articulate that other viewpoint here.

Comparative advantage is no longer the name of our trading game. The managerial powers in the United States have shipped our advantages overseas. They have transferred our capital, our technology, our software and managerial skills to many countries overseas where they have put them together with cheap labor. We no longer have the world's best managers, the world's highest technology, the most capital and the finest, most productive work force. We confront a European community that has organized itself for its own advantage and self-interest. So, too, has Japan, looming large on the economic horizon these last two decades, rolling on and becoming powerful beyond its size or location. We face the command economies of the Eastern European communist nations and now Red China. We deal with developing nations on the move, yearning to reach out for some of the economic advantages they see in the more developed countries.

Above all, since 1973 we confront OPEC. For the first time

a cartel has been created whose every activity has great bearing on the economies of most of the globe's nations and on the lives—the lifestyles—of hundreds of millions of people the world over. In our own country, the last few decades have seen the rise of multinational organizations which deal in self interest against what is often the United States' national interest.

It is within this context that we must consider the Multilateral Trade Negotiations, since those rules will govern international trade for many years. Our judgment must be based on the way the codes will protect American workers and their employers against unfair competition.

We in the Ladies' Garment Workers' Union are in one of the industries that has been most highly affected by the ever-increasing imports of ladies' and children's apparel from the unconscionably low-wage countries overseas. Thus the conduct of the MTN discussions was a matter of grave concern to us when they first began some five years ago. We came pleading to the President and his trade representatives, who agreed that they must not use our products as expendable chips at the horse trading in Geneva by permitting a greater flood of imported textiles and apparel in exchange for promises to buy something else we produced here.

I never deluded myself into thinking we could take textiles, apparel and clothing entirely off the negotiating table in Geneva. We knew it was necessary that we be part of the give and take, but we urged them to give less in the areas of our own parochial interest. While I do not hesitate to call it parochial, I believe that our position was wholly within the national interest. Moreover, I would insist that questions of trade are not to be thought of in the academic or intellectual sense as though they were an exercise in gamesmanship. We are talking about real live human beings. We are talking about jobs, investments and a very wide swath of our economy; one out of every eight industrial jobs is to be found in our industry. All of these things we talk about are national interests.

I do not fault the representatives of Japan, who advocate their own national interests, any more than I would fault any other negotiators, even the group from the European community. But I have found it necessary on occasion to remind our own negotiators of our own national interests.

Let me recall briefly the history of certain earlier trade agreements. In the days of Cordell Hull, we came to our government for special arrangements in the field of cotton and cotton textiles when import penetration began to affect American job opportunities. In 1960-61, under the Kennedy Round, the MFA, a multi-fiber arrangement, was created. Under this orderly marketing procedure we began to negotiate bilateral agreements head to head with specific countries exporting textiles and clothing into the United States. During this time we knew we were riding a tiger. Yet we could not arouse too many of our fellow Americans to understand our interests or even their interests. Our country was going blithely along with only a small percentage of its gross national product in trade. We had a huge domestic market for we had become the world's greatest consumer mass market. We had a jolly old time trading with each other. The small voices of garment workers and textile magnates were not really heard and we were labeled "protectionists," pejoratively.

Bilateral agreements permitted other countries annual increments that increased the amount they could export into the United States by three or four times the increase in domestic growth, demand or consumption. Predictably, they began to take over a larger and larger share of our industry's market. We saw we were going to be consumed by the tiger; at some point domestic industries would have to be at hazard. They would be at hazard because of the great difference between the labor-cost component paid in labor-intensive industries here as against the labor costs of the low-wage exporting countries.

Since the end of the Kennedy Round, world trade has expanded more than six fold. Our country trades more. One of every three acres in the United States produces food or fiber for export. One of every seven manufacturing jobs depends on exports. Unfortunately, however, we import far more than we export. Our negative balance of trade for 1978 was $34 billion, with imported textiles and clothing contributing five billion dollars to that negative balance. But what is much worse is that we have exported more than 500,000 industrial jobs of American workers, jobs we have had in the past as well as jobs we have lost because we never got the advantage of the increase in our own population or the increase in our own standard of living.

What happened to our industry was to happen to other labor-intensive industries in the United States, from shoes to TV sets. As imports are permitted to take over a greater share of each market, factories have been closing all over the country in many industries. Our displaced workers have had no places to go for new jobs.

Who are these people who have lost garment jobs in the United States? They are our own Third World within the borders of the United States, mostly in the big cities—the blacks up from the South, the Hispanics, the Asians, the new immigrants who have come into our country. They are also indigenous Americans in small communities, places with hardly any other economic opportunity once a small plant has shut down owing to the flood of imports.

Because of the history of our union, because of our international outlook, we have already demonstrated an interest in and a caring about workers in the less developed countries. We have already shared to a considerable extent the domestic market that was our own. We are not against sharing our job opportunities. We believe we should permit an increase in the penetration of our market, but only an increase that bears a relationship to the market growth here. We cannot give away all the industrial jobs in the United States.

Under a rational system of fair trade, it may appear reasonable at first analysis that certain labor-intensive work should leave the United States for the low-wage countries of the world: South Korea, the Philippines and the like. Japan, Germany, and the Scandinavian countries have had some success in restructuring a few of their industries that have become noncompetitive in the world community. They have switched workers from some dying industries to sprouting ones. Free traders naturally ask, "If these industrialized countries can effect change with so little trauma, why can't we do the same in the United States?"

The answer is threefold. First, in Japan, Germany and Scandinavia, the people are homogeneous. There is a much higher degree of education and literacy among the workers in all three countries; Japan's literacy rate is almost 100 percent. In contrast, some 23 million in the United States may have serious reading problems while between 18 and 64 million more may be illiterate, according to the latest Ford Foundation study.

Carry-over skills of highly literate people are far superior to those of less literate people. Literate workers are more easily retrainable for higher technology industries. This factor alone makes it easier to move workers in Japan, Germany and Scandinavia from sunset industries into higher-technology sunrise industries. In the United States, our own "Third World" are recent immigrants, often with little or no literacy in any language, much less English. They lack skills of any sort, which makes for greater difficulty in their transfer to higher-technology training and production.

Second, many industrialized countries in Northern Europe invite "guest workers," mostly from Southern Europe, Yugoslavia and Turkey to do the low-paying work. They are almost always sent home when business cycles fall or imports cancel out their jobs. In the United States, all who come have been made welcome, sooner or later. And the way they have gained entry into U.S. industrial life is often through labor-intensive work like textiles, clothing and apparel.

Third, in Japan, Germany and the Scandinavian countries there is a wide community of interest and cooperation among the employer groups, government and organized workers. No such relationship exists here. Even a small attempt by labor unions to reach a national accord on minimum objectives has met with almost total rejection by the business community. Our country has not yet accepted organized labor as a needed, important, integral part of society. I believe such cooperation is the key to the development of any fair policy.

If we could attain a degree of cooperation in the United States among business, labor and government, a willingness to cooperate for the common good, then I could become the "King's First Minister" to aid in liquidating part of our industry. I am not committed to keeping our members in these lowest-paid jobs. On the contrary, I am eager to help them move into better, higher-paying industrial work.

If IBM, GE and other giants would agree to build sizable plants in the South Bronx, Bedford Stuyvesant, Lower Manhattan and other depressed areas throughout the country, and if the government would come in with manpower training programs and a large infusion of money, then our union would immediately plan to funnel people out of the low-paid textile and garment industries into those better jobs. With such planning, we, too, could accomplish what the Japanese, Germans and Scandinavians are beginning to achieve.

Some degree of cooperation among government, business and organized labor seems essential to me if we are to compete in the new economic world of the Tokyo Round. We three can go off in separate directions, or we can go at each other in destructive ways, but our products will be pitted day by day against those made by workers in nations whose disparate interests do pull together for their common good.

The specific codes in the MTN were designed to discourage governments from helping their industries in ways that hurt industries of other countries. How will the AFL-CIO judge the effect of these codes? I think we have some very hard problems. We will be able to evaluate their full impact only with the passage of time. Our judgment must be based on the principle that the codes and implementing legislation must protect American workers and industries against unfair trade competition, to assure a diversified, healthy United States economy as well as a more just society.

Some labor leaders in this country, however, are already disquieted about the codes. I am among those who are uneasy even now. We must, for example, make sure that Section 201 of the Trade Act of 1974 is not affected, because it allows us to conclude orderly agreements in specialty steel, coal, TV, footwear and elsewhere. The public has awakened to the fact that in the last two years these particular products have been heavily impacted by imports. Bilateral arrangements with exporting countries have regulated shipments of these products and helped immensely to sustain U.S. production and employment in these fields.

Let me briefly touch on some of the other codes in the Tokyo Round.

Code on subsidies. Under the terms of this code, subsidies provided to exporters by their governments are acknowledged to give unfair competitive advantage in the marketplace.

In a world where more and more economies are mixed, where many—or often, all—industries are government controlled, the products of our free enterprise system can be undersold unless we can take steps to protect ourselves. Under the code, when subsidies permit foreign firms to sell their goods here at artificially low prices and in the process injure domestic producers, appropriate remedies are provided. A more standardized way to determine injuries is spelled out and the agreement permits our government to impose countervailing duties against injurious imports.

Code on antidumping. When goods are sold here for less than in the home country, or even less than they cost, that is called dumping. The antidumping code will attempt appropriate penalties in the event goods are dumped here.

Code on government purchases. Under this code, contrary to prior practices, governments must open their purchasing to bidders from all countries, subject to some spelled-out limitations. To date, other governments have laws that automatically call for buying their own products and our goods are excluded from their bidding even when we are much more competitive. We have laws, too, about where our government may buy, but with few protections for Made-in-USA products.

I think United States tax dollars should be spent on domestic products. Our laws now enforce the 6 percent to 12 percent preference in minority employment areas or minority and small businesses. If we go along with untrammeled access to our government's procurement, do we turn our back on giving preference in our own country even to small American businesses?

These codes and others, were hammered out with great difficulty by the 99 trading nations, and they may help us; only time will tell. But in my view, they scarcely begin to answer the tough questions facing us.

How, for instance, do we cope with the various mixed economies in the world? Here in the United States we operate within a capitalist system. I wish it were a more free, more democratic and more competitive capitalist system. I am a supporter of this system and I like to see it improve. But we confront an immense challenge as our trading partners begin to evolve systems of mixed economies. Government intervention, financing and ownership are important factors in their economies. How do we cope with it?

As an example, how can the steel industry in the United States remain competitive when it competes not against the British National Steel Corporation but against Great Britain itself, whose national treasury continues to make up the deficits in the manufacture of British steel? And how do we compete against governments like France, which has a large ownership interest in some parts of its economy, which provides a good deal of financing in other parts and which lately has played the leading role in the structural reorganization of some of its industries?

In less developed countries, government interposition and government involvement are growing larger and larger. How do we define these subsidies? How do we compute them? Can the new subsidy and antidumping codes of the Tokyo Round protect us? Are countervailing duties sufficient remedy? Will the rules be interpreted in ways that will help us?

I question the premise that an open trading society is the best society. We need a more rational system of fair trade. A number of developing nations, most particularly China, are going to make extraordinary efforts and extraordinary strides, using largely American capital and American technology, in combination with their very, very low-paid people. Can we provide the necessary jobs to our own people as these countries come onstream?

We are a developed country with a high standard of living

and it is one we want to maintain. We do not earn the highest wages [See Chart Number 2] but we do not want to be averaged out altogether. It has become obvious to us as well as to the European community that restructuring must take place. We no longer make most of our shoes, pocketbooks, TVs or baseball gloves, among many other items. Restructuring will be a trauma for both workers and employers in the sunset industries.

Whatever else might be said about the Multilateral Trade Negotiations, they did serve one useful purpose. They taught us a great deal about the difficulties and dangers in the world trading arena. They helped us understand the myriad problems that have to be confronted, here in the United States and in every country, be it Japan, a developing nation or a state-controlled economy.

In my opinion, the MTN leaves much to be desired, but beyond the MTN only we ourselves, through our own Congress and President, can change those national policies that are harmful to American workers and their employers. I would list these recommendations for national action:

- Regulate the export of American capital and technology. Terminate the Overseas Private Investment Corporation (OPIC), which insures many overseas operations of American multi-national firms.

- Negotiate quotas with our trading partners so that the overseas share of our domestic market in clothing and textiles remains constant.

- Revise or repeal our own tax laws that encourage overseas production.

- Repeal items 806 and 807 of the present United States tariff schedule that reward American companies for production abroad of products intended for sale in the United States.

- Expand generously technical aid to the developing countries for their agricultural development, which will provide their peoples with a healthy economic base and lessen their need to escape into the sweatshops of Third World cities.

- Monitor carefully the interpretations of the anti-dumping subsidies and government purchasing codes as they

Hourly Wages and Fringe Benefits
Apparel*– 1977

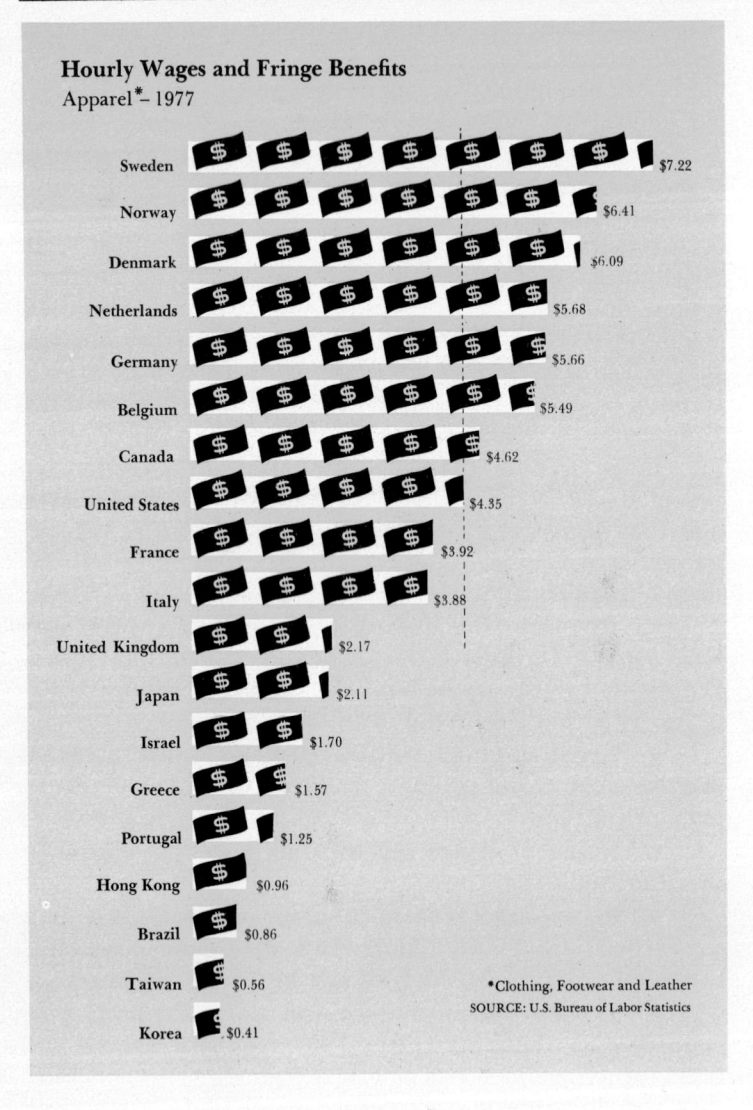

Sweden	$7.22
Norway	$6.41
Denmark	$6.09
Netherlands	$5.68
Germany	$5.66
Belgium	$5.49
Canada	$4.62
United States	$4.35
France	$3.92
Italy	$3.88
United Kingdom	$2.17
Japan	$2.11
Israel	$1.70
Greece	$1.57
Portugal	$1.25
Hong Kong	$0.96
Brazil	$0.86
Taiwan	$0.56
Korea	$0.41

*Clothing, Footwear and Leather
SOURCE: U.S. Bureau of Labor Statistics

Chart Number 2

appear.

- Encourage increase in capital investment here in the United States through judicious use of tax credits.
- Research productivity to assure the maintenance of high levels of efficiency.
- Improve trade adjustment assistance to help alleviate the immediate hardship of job loss due to imports.
- Establish a national commission of diverse interests in the United States to help formulate a comprehensive approach to problems arising from our trade relationships.

These are among the issues we must debate over the next decade. Our efforts to rationalize our own industries will have to begin; MTN forces that upon us. We have the time and if we have the will, we surely have the intelligence, creativity, technological know-how and money to find humane and appropriate solutions. But time runs out. Our workers and their families should not—cannot—afford the terrible burdens they will bear tomorrow if we fail them today.

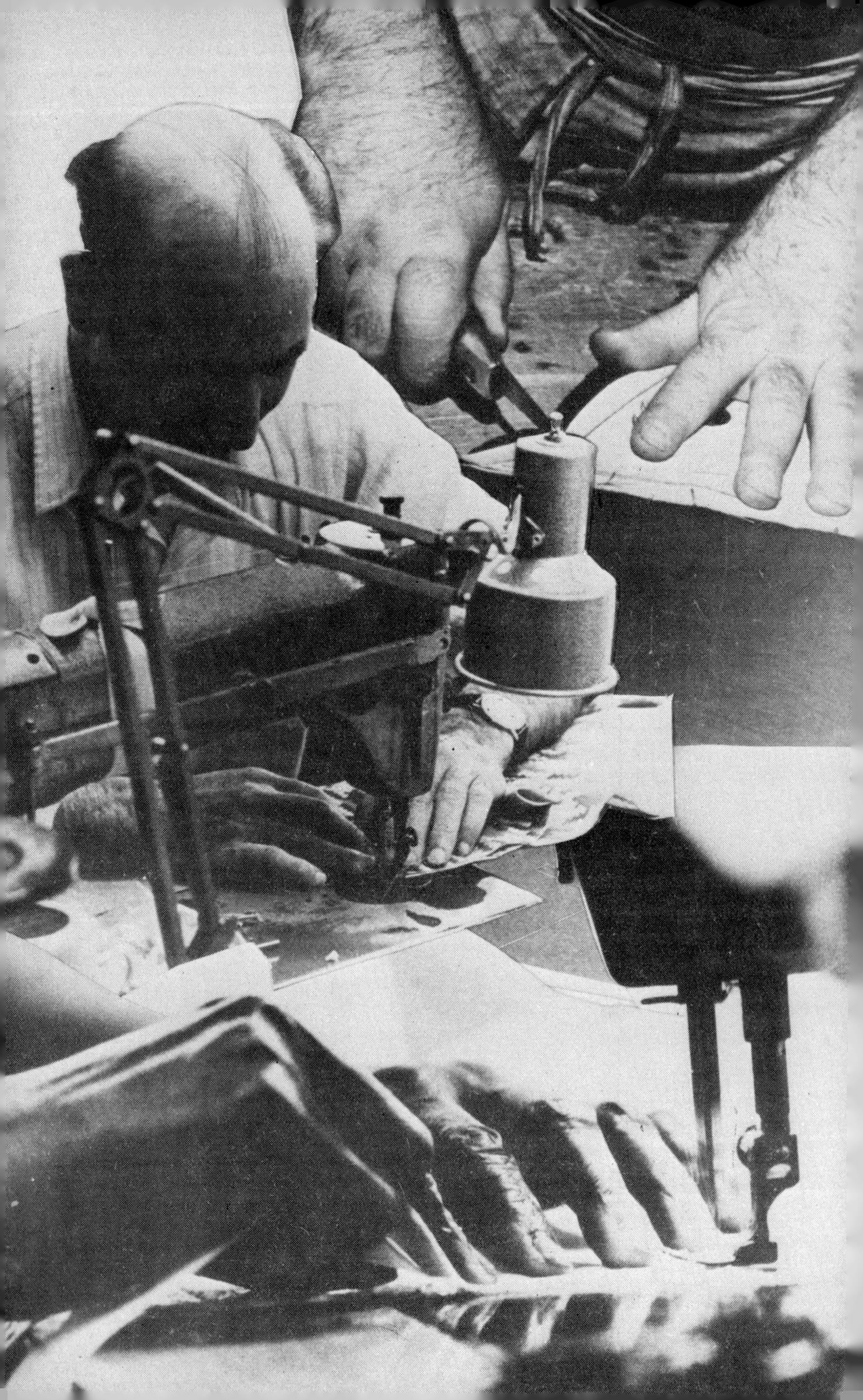

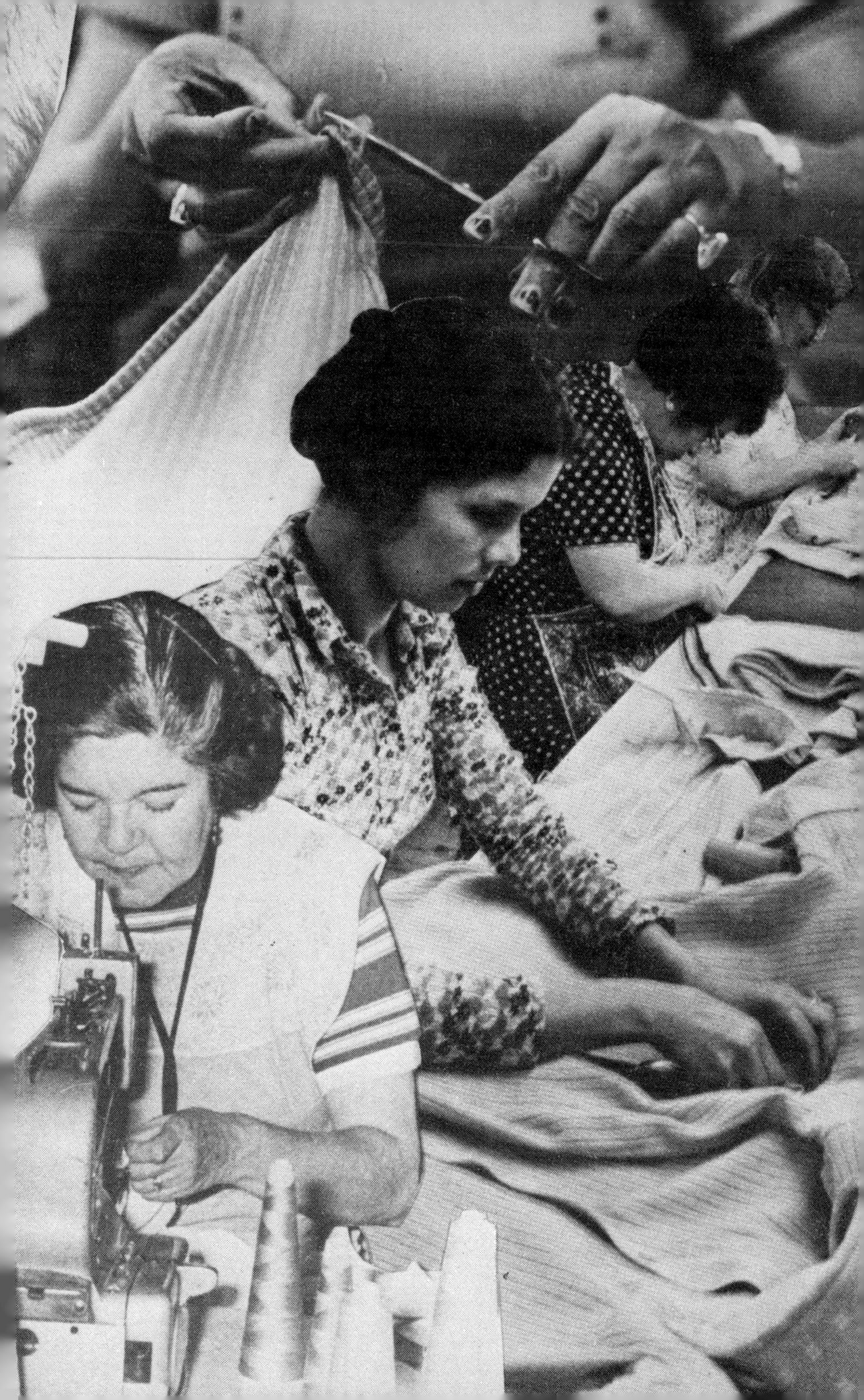

part two

SOCIAL UNIONISM

Striving for better wages, better working conditions, better benefits, wanting "More!"—that's unionism. But the ILG, from its very first day, has struggled for more than "More!"

We are a union dedicated to the welfare of our members—the way our children are educated, the manner in which community services are developed and delivered. We are a union dedicated to political democracy without which we could not survive, a union dedicated to that better life and that better world which each of us seeks for ourselves—more than that, for our children and most of all, for our grandchildren. We know that their happiness and ours depends upon our working for the welfare of all people, in a just and equitable society. That's social unionism.

Sol Chick Chaikin

one

Organized Labor: Its Historic Role

Weinberg Seminar,
Cornell University, Ithaca, N.Y., November 13, 1978.

To many Americans, the term *union* conjures up a single behemoth. In actuality, organized labor is made up of an assortment of unions whose differing styles and disparate histories reflect their memberships and problems.

In U.S. unionism there is unexpected variety. Meek company unions unattached to any national group are formed, to all appearances, to rubber stamp company policy; these are not even considered labor unions by either the National Labor Relations Board or the Bureau of Labor Statistics. Militant unions are aggressive in their push for more and more.

Chaikin uses a venerable term, *social unionism*, to describe the philosophy of the ILGWU and unions like it.

Cornell is the home of the New York State School of Industrial and Labor Relations, which sponsors the Weinberg Seminars. This speech was given at the 20th such seminar to representatives from management, government and education. "Management's Historic Role and Future Mission" was examined by William May, chairman of the American Can Company. Chaikin's assigned topic was "Labor's Historic Role and Future Mission."

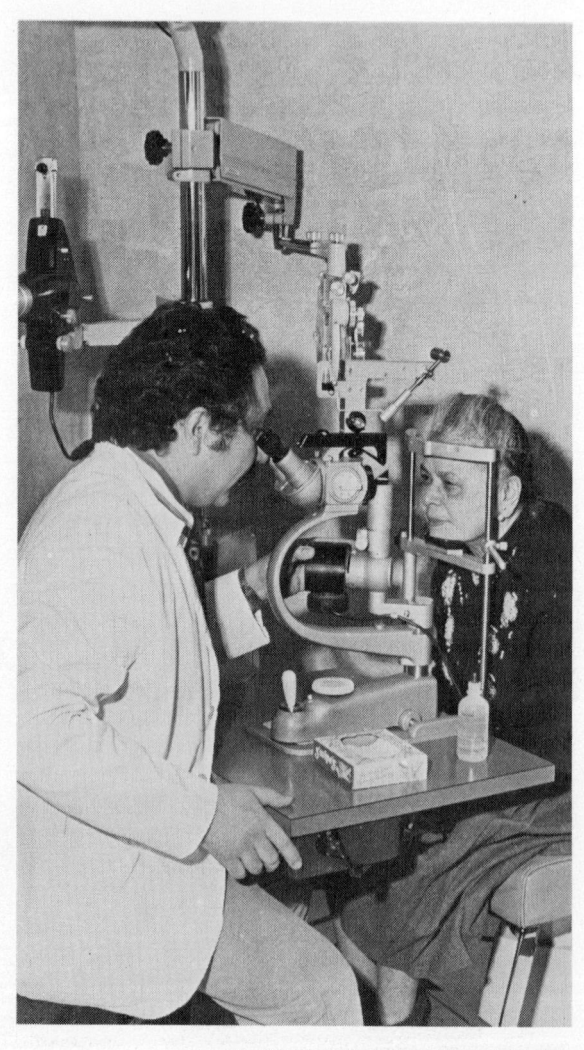

ILGWU Health Center, New York City

All too often, the news of a breach of union trust committed by a single union official blackens tens of thousands of incorruptible union people with that mean stereotype. Somehow, when a dishonest banker is uncovered, Americans do not tar all other bankers with his crooked brush. It may surprise you to learn that union officials generally are far, far more honest than bankers, and I can prove that bald statement. The cost for my union to bond me is much, much lower than it is for any of you gentlemen or lady bankers who are present today—and bondsmen know.

Confronted by the enormous inconveniences of garbage piling up in the streets because government workers are out on strike, Americans are likely to conclude that all unions are strike-happy. This is not the case. Each year the overwhelming number of wage negotiations are settled without loss of production. When a wage settlement is believed to be too generous, or when it seems as though unions battle to protect jobs by overloading makework—featherbedding—many Americans are persuaded that we in labor are a grasping lot, that we exist solely for parochial, narrow self-interest. The history of the American labor movement belies these stereotypes. Unfortunately, our history is not as well-known as it should be.

I would like to describe the role I believe the organized labor movement has played in this country and the contributions it has made to the well-being of all Americans.

As industrial citizens of this country, our historic mission has been to organize the unorganized. From the moment two people employed by a third person discovered they had a common interest, they attempted to share their weaknesses, merge their strengths, pool their courage, unite their aspirations, and combine their objectives. Our mission has been to provide the vehicle by which workers—badly outweighed in terms of bargaining strength and organization—might redress the balance, might have something to say about what their time, their skill and their dedication to the job were worth.

As a result of the trade union movement, many workers have gone a fair distance toward this objective. Moreover, higher wage standards, which evolved because of union organization and the collective bargaining process, have helped the U.S. community in many ways. Higher wages provided a market for mass production because more money was placed in the hands of consumers who then went into the marketplace to buy goods. This increase in demand gave tremendous impetus to American entrepreneurs to provide more goods and services, which in turn spurred other advances, creating the catalyst for managerial ingenuity, scientific brilliance and technological genius. The result has been, except for certain by-passed persons in our society, that people in the United States have enjoyed a higher standard of living.

In addition, there have been spin-offs in physical, social and cultural attainments. American workers, able to earn enough to support themselves by working fewer hours in a day and fewer days in a week, have had more time for leisure—for sports, for travel, for the appreciation and support of the arts. They have generated more tax money to finance the performing arts.

This country's free trade union movement was never satisfied with concentrating simply on wages and hours. When my father joined the union it was not only to get another penny an hour. He saw unions as a vehicle for change, for social justice, tolerance, decency and economic security: a way to change the world.

Major elements within our movement have always been concerned with the way our members live as citizens, with the type of schools our children go to, with the kind of houses our members live in, and with the government services that are made available at the local, state and national levels. So it is that, once they join the union and become full industrial citizens, we talk with our people about the necessity of becoming political citizens. We have always held that a man or woman who joined a union to have something to say about wages, hours and working conditions did not become a full citizen of the United States until he or she became concerned with the manner in which the nation was governed. We preach the need for union members to become political citizens.

Since an informed voter strengthens the democratic process, we have urged Americans inside and outside of unions to gain knowledge. We were the first in the United States to argue for free, universal, public school education. This was a major tenet of working men's parties back in 1823-1832. Beyond that, trade unions went on to argue for creation of vocational and intermediate schools, and for free colleges. Our vision always included access to knowledge for U.S. workers.

We were in the vanguard of those who argued that senators of the United States should be elected at large by the voters of each state rather than be appointed or elected by state legislatures.

We have argued vociferously for the extension of voting rights. We were among the first in this country to demand the abolition of poll taxes, a device employed in many communities to restrict the ballot to the rich and well-born.

We were in the forefront of the effort to curb literacy tests, which were used to deny some Americans the opportunity to participate in the political life of their communities. We argue to this very day for liberalized registration. In some jurisdictions the technical requirements for registration and eligibility to vote are plainly designed to exclude new voters and thereby preserve the status quo. We joined with others in the community to extend the right to vote to 18-year-olds because it was our conviction that at 18, a person had sufficient maturity to make reasonable judgments in elections. We led the fight for the open primary, to take politics out of party conventions and to the people.

We in the trade union movement have fought vigorously to advance the practice of one person, one vote so there would no longer be rotten boroughs, where a representative in the state house or in Washington could have the same vote in the lower house as another representative chosen by three, four or five times as many voters.

As part of our concept of political citizenship we turned to the question of taxes. We argued that taxes should be collected fairly through a progressive tax system. The first federal income tax law in this country was based to a large extent on that theory.

We thought not only of our members' needs as industrial and political citizens, but also of their health, of the need to deliver quality medical care to every American as his or her birthright. No American, we have always believed, should ever know anything so horrendous as the inability of a mother to bring a sick child to a doctor because she had no money to pay. Through collective bargaining agreements, some unions have negotiated benefits that enable them to create health and medical centers for their members. Out of intense negotiations, from agreements reaching back 50 to 60 years, we have been major contributors to the great system of third-party medicine in America.

We in the labor movement were always concerned about the conditions under which our members worked in the shops, in the mines, in the mills, on the docks. The question of shop sanitation may be taken for granted by some today, but in the early years of this country, very few employers gave a thought to sanitary facilities, to such ordinary working conditions as good light, fresh air and ready escape in case of fire. In the late 1800s and early 1900s, the workplace was usually dank, dark and dangerous. The union movement struggled bitterly to make the workplace cleaner, safer and more decent.

In spite of our progress, the problem is still with us. Just think of a disease such as brown lung, byssinosis, to which workers in textile factories are prone, or of black lung, to which miners have been subjected. Consider the horrible dangers of cancer-causing environments to asbestos workers, and to those who handle nuclear and hydrocarbon materials.

We attacked the problem of poverty early on. Indeed, the very existence of labor unions is a major force in the fight against poverty. We attempt to get for workers a little better wage, a little better job security, a little better protection against the ravages of illness or accident; those are all major contributing forces in the fight against poverty.

We went to the community to argue—in most cases

successfully—for the establishment of minimum wages, so that people who did not benefit from union organization, who were absolutely at the mercy of their employers, would have some help in the form of legislation. Similarly, we were among the first to bring to the attention of the community and the lawmakers the primitiveness of the common-law view of injury on the job. It wrought havoc upon American wage earners injured at work. We supported safety legislation and we were the ones who proposed and supported workmen's compensation to provide a modicum of help to the worker injured or disabled on the job and to the widow and children of a worker killed on the job.

We in organized labor were the primary force behind the establishment of a system of unemployment compensation. For years we struggled to provide a measure of decency to the thousands, hundreds of thousands and millions of workers thrown out of work by the business cycles of the capitalist system.

Most trade union leaders were committed to the idea of Social Security and provided the leadership that finally achieved it. We were united in the belief that a democracy could not survive merely because its people could register and vote, but would endure only when, in addition, a decent reward was paid to those among us who had the least, who, for whatever reason, could not survive without the help of the rest of us.

Throughout the years, one primary human need has been housing. Unions used their own creativity and their own capital investment to become pioneers in the field of cooperative housing for workers. We petitioned our political leaders to think of contributions the community could make to provide proper housing for the many among us who could not afford it.

We were also involved in one of the most important struggles in the American experience—the fight to assure each human being, regardless of race, creed, color or national origin, a full and fair opportunity for schooling, for housing, for equality before the law. There were some unions, reflecting prejudices of their day, that accepted only Caucasians, but this practice was far from universal in the trade union movement. To the credit of U.S. unions, differences among them were aired, fights lost one day were resumed the next day, or the next month or year. The battles that took place at conventions of union leaders on questions of equal rights occurred earlier, were more advanced, and more intense than the discussions in the general community.

During the war years, some unions in the AFL were among the groups that persuaded President Roosevelt to issue the now-famous executive order on fair employment practices. We continued that campaign right through the civil rights fights of the 1960s. In 1964 we were deeply involved in the battle for the Voting Rights Act. We have been strongly committed to passage of the Equal Rights Amendment. Even today we pursue the struggle for economic opportunity for all, pressuring many of our union leaders to change their attitudes and their performance, and to establish union outreach programs.

Our concern has extended to working people beyond our borders. Our solidarity with workers overseas goes back at least to 1919 when Sam Gompers, the first AFL president, proposed the formation of the ILO, the International Labor Organization, to improve workers' lives worldwide. Despite our temporary departure from the ILO we have maintained an abiding interest in all international workers' movements based on democratic principles. In the middle 1930s, when most Americans either did not know or hid from knowledge of the effects of Mussolini and Hitler, the AFL, aided by a number of CIO unions, raised money to assist democratic elements in Nazi Germany and Fascist Italy. An underground railroad of sorts was created to help democrats, political leaders, and trade unionists to escape. The Jewish Labor Committee performed similar work for the threatened Jewish communities. Unions also started the Anti-Nazi Non-Sectarian League long before the United States recognized the extraordinary threat to our national interests posed by the gathering storm in Europe.

After the Second World War, the AFL and the CIO were among the leading supporters of overseas aid. We helped spearhead the drive for the Marshall Plan, for food grants and for grants-in-aid. Today we argue for special assistance for developing nations to enable them to feed themselves while they industrialize.

We also helped form the International Confederation of Free Trade Unions, ICFTU, of which we were a leading member for many years. We still maintain ties in the regional groupings with representatives of trade union movements, some free and many not so free. Individually, unions are members of international trade secretariats, where workers of industrialized nations and developing nations meet to talk about their common problems. Through a myriad of regional, bilateral and multilateral relationships, the delegates of the AFL-CIO, which represent the largest, strongest free trade union center in the world, are able to make judgments on how to aid workers and unions in other lands, always with the aim of advancing the democratic spirit.

In short, union contributions in domestic affairs and foreign relations have been many and decisive. They have been achieved by the dedication and sacrifices of countless millions of working Americans in the trade union movement, often against great opposition. Our contributions have aided the well being of all Americans because never have our objectives been so narrow or parochial as to include benefits only for ourselves. We have a long and honorable history of acting to relieve the nation's social problems, and if we are often alone in our battles at their beginnings, we have had the satisfaction of finding the rest of the community supporting us when the victories have come.

two

ILG: A Special Union In A Unique Industry

**Fashion Institute of Technology,
New York, N.Y., October 23, 1978.**

The ILGWU has had a long association with the Fashion Institute of Technology. Chaikin is a trustee, as were the two previous presidents, Louis Stulberg and David Dubinsky. F.I.T.'s student center is named in honor of David Dubinsky.

The International Ladies' Garment Workers' Union was founded in 1900 by 11 workers who met on June 3 as delegates from four cities, Baltimore, Philadelphia, Newark and New York. They represented about 2000 workers from seven unions, each of which was assessed $10 to create a fund with which to begin the work of the new organization. Dues were set at 1 cent per member per week. Canadian delegates were invited to the founding convention and although unable to attend, did join later. The immigrants who founded the ILG came to the United States primarily from eastern Europe, followed quite rapidly by others from southern Europe. These Jews and Italians arrived yearning to breathe freely, seeking to practice their religion without hindrance, hoping for a chance to live a little better.

Stories of the great United States with its golden opportunities had percolated up and wafted overseas to the small secluded villages of many countries. People of varying backgrounds flocked to these shores. They were frustrated writers, artists and musicians, some intellectuals, some craftsmen, some farmers. Many spoke more than one language, often three or four. Most came to this great country only to find themselves without any training or useful preparation for the kind of life that existed here.

By the turn of the century New York had plenty of jobs for immigrants in the new and burgeoning apparel industry. At one time, wealthier people had had their clothes made by seamstresses in their immediate employ, women who were part of the household help. Then the business of ready-made clothes came into being; clothes became cheaper and more available. Factories sprang up to make these much-wanted items, factories eager and able to absorb tens of thousands, even hundreds of thousands of the new immigrants.

But the workers found themselves in what was then commonly known as sweatshops: miserable places where people sweated or shivered from sunrise past sunset. During the early years tuberculosis ran rampant among garment workers, who labored in close, fetid quarters where fresh air could not penetrate, with hardly sufficient light to see the ends of their fingers, where the needle, thread and thimble coincided.

That was when the ILGWU was born. There were no protective labor laws in those days, no standards for safety or sanitation, no standards for light, air or quick exits. There was no legislation protecting human beings who had to work for a living, nothing to interpose itself between the employer and the employee. The worker was utterly helpless because new waves of immigrants followed one upon the other, providing always a surplus of labor. If anyone complained, someone else was all too desperate to fill that place.

In 1900, under those conditions of great despair and distress, without the protection of labor laws, workers pledged their common courage and strength to join in union to improve their wages, hours and conditions of work.

Our union's struggles are replete with stories of coming together, of sacrifices, sometimes with only a small measure of

Gibson Girls—1895
Artist: Charles Bana
Photo:
Bettman Archives.

success. Early on, workers would struggle to move forward to better wages and conditions, then something would intervene to weaken the union. It was an example of the way human progress has been made since time immemorial—two steps forward, a step and a half back, sometimes a push to the side. But if you measure our life span from one decade to another, steady and inexorable progress was made.

    The winter of 1909-1910 was a landmark in the history of the ILGWU and a landmark as well in both the history of the American labor movement and the women's movement. Tens of thousands of women had come into the garment industry, previously dominated by male workers, to sew shirtwaists, those grand blouses made popular by the drawings of the Gibson Girl. They were exploited—terribly, horribly exploited in the sweat shops of New York, Philadelphia, Boston and Baltimore. Finally, 20,000 of them, thinly clad, poorly fed, joined together on the bitter winter streets to protest the inhumane conditions under which they were forced to work. It was the first large-scale women's strike in America and, against brutal police, scabs and very great odds, they won it. Over 300 shops were converted into full union contract shops. Thousands of shirt-waist makers, 80 percent of them women, joined this union in one great ingathering.

Within five months there was a massive strike in the ladies' coat and suit industry. Not to be outdone by the women, 60,000 workers took to the streets, mostly men, the greatest outpouring of workers in any trade that had ever been seen. That violence-filled strike was helped to a settlement by a lawyer, Louis Brandeis, who later became one of the finest justices of the United States Supreme Court. His creative intelligence provided an arbitration clause in the collective bargaining agreement that ended the strike. It was a first in the history of labor relations in the United States. Up to that time when an argument between an employer and the union could not be resolved through discussion, compromise, or agreement, only two paths had been open. One was for the employer to lock out the workers, to send them out and not permit them to work; the other was for the union to declare a strike and ask workers to leave their jobs. In both cases there was loss of production, loss of wages and loss of strength to each party in the dispute. Even when the union had to strike because of inhumane conditions and improvements resulted, workers could still emerge greatly weakened. Brandeis helped create the mechanism for arbitration and peaceful settlement of labor disputes. It was the first of its kind and pointed the way for other unions.

After the first World War, the union faced the regressive attitudes of tough employers who had grown bigger and richer as a result of war industries and chose to battle back viciously. Workers everywhere were struggling against exploitation and were forming other unions. The 1920s was an unsettled period for labor and we in the ILGWU suffered along with our brothers and sisters in other industries.

We suffered also because of an attack on our union from a wholly different quarter, a takeover attempt by some workers within and outside our own ranks who were sold the communist idea. In Russia a communist revolution deposed the czar and swept away the existing institutions, grafting a whole new way of life onto Russian society. As ideas know no boundaries, that ideology floated over to the United States and was convincing to some workers in the ILGWU who, embracing the newly-founded Communist Party, attempted to take over. In 1926 they gained control of the New York Cloak Joint Board and declared a general strike in New York City, which spread dissension and bankrupted the union. Eventually, the democratic elements regained control, but by then our union was weak and without money. We attempted to re-establish ourselves, only to be confronted with the great depression of 1929 that lasted until the United States entered the Second World War.

Throughout, we have struggled to maintain our standards, to get for the workers in this industry an opportunity to live a little better and to share more equitably the wealth they help to produce. Moreover, we have tried to maintain a reasonably cooperative attitude towards the employers with whom we have dealt because we knew early on that ours was a unique kind of industry.

Ours is not an industry with huge companies like U.S. Steel, which has its workers organized in the United Steel Workers of America; or like General Motors and their United Automobile Workers of America. We are not the kind of industry that comes to mind when you think of a tremendous corporate goliath like the American Telephone and Telegraph Company, which in effect is a pure and simple monopoly, with the Telephone Workers Union or the Communications Workers Union of America confronting tremendous concentrations of capital.

By and large, we are an industry of small entrepreneurs, an industry that developed as perhaps the last bastion of free, competitive, democratic capitalism in this country. Instead of 20 individual employers who might create a measure of competition, or 200 employers or 2,000 who would multiply the competition, all making garments of every type and description, there are more than 20,000 individual employers in this country, each fighting for a share of the consumer's dollar. Instead of goliaths like the huge corporations that employ 50,000 or 150,000 workers, or, in the case of A.T.&T., hundreds of thousands of workers under one corporate roof, our employers engage 15, 115, 215, perhaps 515 workers. Only a very, very few apparel companies employ as many as 1000 workers; very rarely do they employ more. The average firm in our industry employs 50 production workers.

Think of the volume of sales of the giant American corporations, one billion dollars a year or more. In the ladies' and children's apparel industry, the jurisdiction covered by the ILGWU, hardly one company approaches 500 million dollars of sales per year. The average gross income of our typical employer barely exceeds two to three million per year, something like a small supermarket.

I am describing small entrepreneurs, truly competitive entrepreneurs, under-capitalized entrepreneurs. Our recognition of these facts gives rise to a special way of dealing with our employers. A certain community of interest exists between us in the sense that very often what is good for the employer can be good for the worker. Nevertheless, there is inevitable confrontation between union and management: there are differences; there are arguments. Yet we have evolved a way of resolving these differences without doing too much harm to each other. Sometimes we argue, sometimes we strike—although there has not been a major strike in our industry since 1958. Whatever the problem, we negotiate with the understanding, unspoken though it may be, that we must not do too much damage to each other. Neither the union nor the employers are strong enough to sustain such damage.

Eventually, the ILG grew to about 460,000 members, respectable in size, very strong in spirit. What made our restraint remarkable was the fact that our union was then and still is stronger than any single employer or reasonable combination of employers. When a union has that kind of position in an industry, it has to inhibit itself, to control itself, to say to itself once in a while, "Be careful. Don't push your weight around unduly." We have been very sensitive about our position in the industry and have tried to relate to the position of the employers with whom we deal.

This is an industry that gives people an opportunity for tremendous creative development, which is why you are all here studying at the Fashion Institute of Technology. The industry feeds upon creativity and it should compete on that basis. The competitive edge must not be achieved on the backs of the workers. We try not to create a circumstance where one employer is more successful because he pays less to workers than do his competitors; he should not have to grind a human being down to stay in business. We urge our employers to compete with one another in their merchandising practices, their ways of making style seem exciting. We encourage them to compete with each other in fashion sense, understanding which fabrics and colors are suitable for their designs and divining which fashions will sell. There is plenty of room for competition because we have an enormous market to serve, the richest in the world.

From about 1890 until after the Second World War, New York City was the center of fashion and production in our industry. Garment making had centered here because labor came to this city first from Europe, was cheap, plentiful and exploitable. It blossomed here and the management of it has remained here for the same reason you came to study in the "Big Apple" and not in Oshkosh, Wisconsin or Birmingham, Alabama. You came because of the concentration of genius here; you are attracted by the excitement of a major city. Excitement and genius are what generates fashion. Skills came to the fore here, skills not of workers alone, but also of management, of designers, piece-goods buyers, merchandisers, and, something you may not think of, the financial skills of those who loaned money. Without the unique banking interests in this great city of ours, no garment industry could have survived for long.

Every part of the garment industry needs financing. In our industry, designers plan six months or more in advance of the selling season, depending on the type of garment and the

styling that goes into it. Since most management principals are under capitalized, they must have access to special banking, to loans that can tide them over until they design their lines, purchase fabrics, make patterns, cut piece goods, get their workers to sew it, inspect it, pack it, and ship it. Then they keep their fingers crossed and wait thirty to sixty days before the retailer sends them the money for that shipment. During this period of many, many months, employers need the financing to carry them, and New York, of course, was and is the financial center of the world.

So it was that the industry settled in New York; here we had all the necessities. There were garment factories in places like Chicago, Louisville and San Francisco from the earliest years but the vast number were in this area. New York remained queen bee of the manufacture of apparel until profound changes came to the United States. In 1928, 12 out of 15 of our members still lived and worked here; today only 5 out of 15 production workers are employed here. Easy communications became widespread, transportation grew better and people were able to go from one place to another very quickly. Trucks that used to take days to go from New York City to Pennsylvania could now go overnight on the new superhighways.

Labor surplus areas opened up elsewhere-in the country. For example, in the 1920s and 1930s runaway textile mills from Massachusetts fled to the South looking for cheap labor, leaving behind hundreds of thousands of workers with little or nothing to do. Garment manufacturers began to find their way to the old empty mills in Massachusetts. Some of them stopped in Connecticut on their way up. Something similar was happening in the hard-coal mining areas of Pennsylvania as anthracite was utilized less and less. People started using oil because it was easier to handle, cleaner and cheaper. As the coal mines shut down throwing the men out of work, their wives, daughters and sisters became available for low-paid work in garment shops.

Relocating the garment industry was not difficult since it is an industry on wheels. It can be moved overnight because capital investment is low, machines are easily transportable and materials are comparatively light. Clothes are not steel, not copper, not lumber, not cement, not brick.

Factories moved from New York and spread out. First they crept out to the Northeast, primarily into New Jersey, Connecticut, Massachusetts and Pennsylvania, then further south and further west, always in search of cheaper, more exploitable labor. In this most competitive capitalist industry, employers were not content to compete against each other with their styling, their merchandising, their fabrics, their colors. They thought that, in addition, they ought to have the opportunity to compete on the backs of the workers: Find a place where workers can be more exploited and you have higher profits.

Wherever the garments may be made, whether in Mississippi, Arizona, California, the Bronx, or Illinois, those garments are sold in a national market. Retailers, the big department stores and their buying offices, big chains like Sears, J.C. Penney, Montgomery Ward and the great discount houses—all of them shop in a national market. They do not ask, "Is this garment made in New York or in Mississippi? Is it made by a union member or by a non-union worker? Is it made by a worker who earns $5.50 an hour and has an opportunity to feed his family, or is it made by a worker who does not make even $2.65 [minimum wage in 1978] and barely has an opportunity to stay alive? These questions are not of concern in the national market.

As garment factories abandoned New York, we in the ILG followed the bundles of work to bring the message of unionism to the new workers in outlying areas. We had a large measure of success. We discovered that workers in Massachusetts and Pennsylvania were generally the same. They wanted to have something to say about the value of their work, their time and their sweat. They wanted to have something to say about their self-respect and dignity, their wages, working conditions and job security. Today, we have members in 38 states out of the 50, in four provinces of Canada and in Puerto Rico.

While the employers were running away to low-wage areas in the United States and Puerto Rico, a new problem presented itself, caused by the same factors that had led to the dispersal of the industry outside New York. The craft of making garments is not a closely-kept secret. The technology of making clothes—the machines used, the managerial know-how necessary to run these plants—is not kept locked up from public view. It is not copyrighted, patented or restricted, as computer technology may be. All the expertise that goes into our industry is readily available to anybody who wants to reach out and use it.

The employers of this industry, ever searching for advantages, began now to look for exploitable workers in other countries. More and more countries became free and sovereign powers, out from under the yoke of imperial powers like Great Britain, Germany, France, Italy, Holland or Belgium. These independent nations had only one real asset, their poor, very poor people who desperately needed something to do. They were trainable. They had the average coordination of hand, eye and mind that this industry requires. They could learn by precept and example. They would work for little or nothing. I mean almost literally nothing, even less than a nickel or a dime an hour. Our industry, which was already so excessively competitive and cutthroat, became even more difficult for the workers here who were struggling to do well. The import penetration into our domestic market is now extraordinary. For every 100 pieces of all women's and children's clothes made in the United States, there are 38 pieces imported.

What is the disparity in wages today? In New York City the average wage of our workers is approximately $5.00 or $5.50 an hour, the highest wages in the American apparel industry. The further south you go or the further west you go the average wage declines so that the country's average is about $4.25 an hour. Today in Taiwan the average wage of a garment worker is hardly 40 cents an hour. In Hong Kong, it approaches 80 cents, while in Singapore it is 29 cents. In Bangladesh the wage is 16 cents an hour and in India it is hardly more than that. *[For other wage comparisons, see Chart Number 2 on Page 86.]*

Some of you young people know what Calcutta cloth is. You have seen the gauzy, filmy blouses, some with embroidery, that may have been done by hand or machine. You will not be happy to learn that some Indian woman who sat and worked long, long hours hardly earned ten to twelve cents an hour doing it. If she worked a 10 hour day, perhaps she earned a whole dollar and a half; she may have earned only a single dollar. This is the kind of competition American industry faces. It causes very grave problems.

Why do I tell you all this? I tell it to you because we in the ILG depend in major part on young creative people, people like yourselves with fresh ideas. This industry lives on style and fashion. Fresh ideas and new styling are essential to keep alive an interest in the products we make. Success in style determines the availability of work for our members. When and if you do become a designer's assistant, and then a designer, your creativity will be vital to us.

Not many of you will become members of the ILG—only those of you who become sample hands, cutters, pattern graders or pattern makers. Many of you are studying in this fine institution because you want to work in designing, merchandising, textiles, manufacturing or sales. You may go into fashion advertising or into distribution. Those are crafts and skills beyond the immediate purview of our union. Some of you may become part of the management of the productive process. You will have learned something about economics, something about the principles of management. You may even have developed some prejudices against unions, so we want you to know something about us. We want you to know we are not just a name in the paper, some initials used loosely. The ILGWU is made up of real live human beings who have extraordinary problems daily: finding jobs, working steadily, trying to get decent pay to support families and keep them together. We want you to know that in this U.S. economy, our members earn far less than the average industrial wage.

We welcome you and we need you. We need your talent, commitment, and adventurous approach to this industry, just as you need our hands, dedication and skilled workmanship. When you make it, give a thought to those of us who are struggling daily in the factories of this nation.

three

The Two-Tier Society Of The United States

A.

Our Two-Tier Labor Force

**Work in America Institute,
New York, N.Y., March 4, 1979.**

> The term *union member* seems to suggest that America's organized working class, like homogenized milk, is the same from top to bottom. In reality the labor movement is not evenly constituted. At the top, organized workers earn creditable wages and benefits. At the bottom, income is inadequate on all counts.
>
> In the following remarks, Chaikin distinguishes the groups within the labor force, both organized and unorganized.

I do not speak on behalf of all labor, nor can anyone. Our movement is far from homogeneous; we are not all alike. We do not think alike nor do we confront the same problems. In my judgment there are two separate and distinct groups of workers in this country: the "haves" and the "have-nots." The two groups are

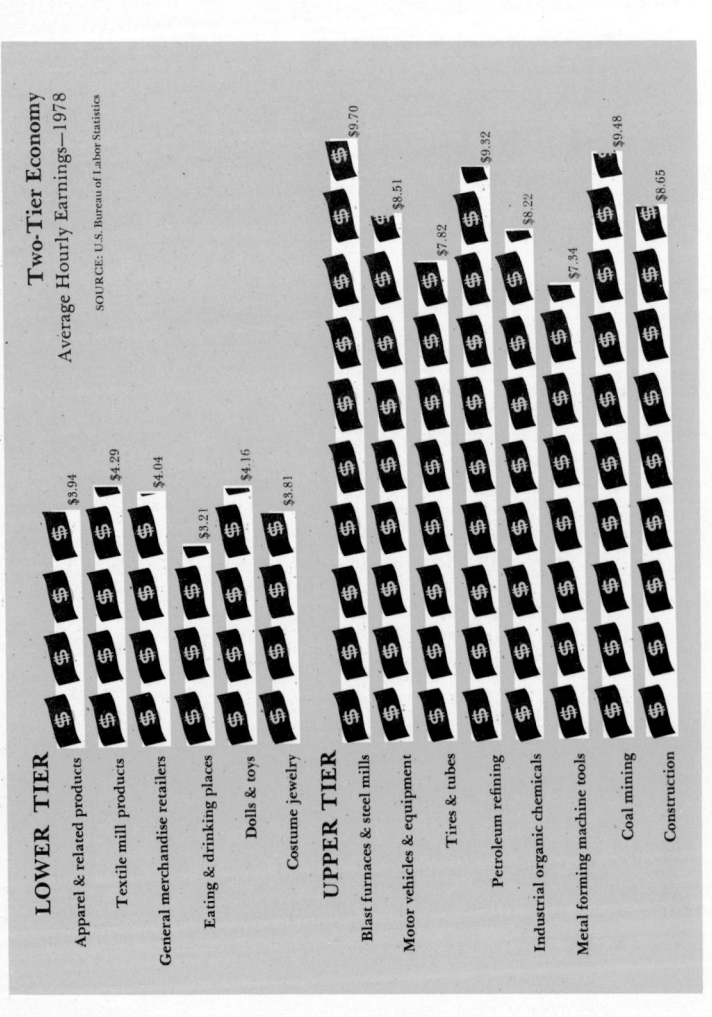

Chart Number 3

Two-Tier Economy
Average Hourly Earnings—1978

SOURCE: U.S. Bureau of Labor Statistics

LOWER TIER

Industry	Hourly Earnings
Apparel & related products	$3.94
Textile mill products	$4.29
General merchandise retailers	$4.04
Eating & drinking places	$3.21
Dolls & toys	$4.16
Costume jewelry	$3.81

UPPER TIER

Industry	Hourly Earnings
Blast furnaces & steel mills	$9.70
Motor vehicles & equipment	$8.51
Tires & tubes	$7.82
Petroleum refining	$9.92
Industrial organic chemicals	$8.22
Metal forming machine tools	$7.34
Coal mining	$9.48
Construction	$8.65

represented even inside unions.

Within organized labor itself there are the "haves" or what I call the "first tier" workers. These include members in such industries as steel, copper, autos and tires; those engaged in defense-related industries, oil, industrial chemicals and aerospace; certain workers in the machine tool industries; mining, construction and some categories of public employees. There are millions of such organized workers. They are in industries averaging 8 to 10 dollars an hour in wages; they earn perhaps $16,000 a year or more. They enjoy worker benefits that can add from 45 to 60 percent to their wages. These "haves" deal mostly with employers in highly technologically-advanced industries that usually have large capital investments; to increase productivity, they are often engaged in research and development, sometimes at taxpayer expense. [*See Chart Number 3.*]

Though there are certain shadings, I call the "have-nots" the "second tier." Within the AFL-CIO they include service workers; most workers in the textile and clothing industry; those in retail establishments; others in certain durable goods like furniture; those who make costume jewelry, toys, dolls and sportsgoods; in short, workers who for the most part are in labor-intensive industries where labor is more important than capital, where there is generally little capital tied up in equipment and where there is hardly any private money for research or development and never any government money. There are uncounted millions more "have-nots" than "haves." Many of them are also members of well-organized unions, but they average only about $5.00 an hour with far fewer benefits. Many earn less than $10,000 a year because they often do not work full time.

The majority of workers in the United States are unorganized, some 60 millions. They, too, fall into two distinct groups. Among the "haves" are the skilled workers, often in great demand. Riding on union coattails without paying their dues, many workers earn close to union wages because what a union gains in wages often sets the pay standards for the whole area since collective bargaining, not individual bargaining, is the best way yet devised for workers to move ahead. But as a general rule the unorganized "haves" gain few union worker benefits, thus falling short of the organized first tier in the total package.

Then there are the unorganized "have-nots." The legally lowest-paid workers in the land are those earning minimum wages or less. When labor convinces Congress once every three or four years to increase the federal national minimum wage, some otherwise reasonably well-informed citizens learn, for the first time, that 5 to 5½ million Americans depend, almost entirely, on an increase in the national minimum wage law for a little better break from this economy of ours.

Moreover, minimum wage workers receive almost nothing over and above the wage rate in the form of benefits or other advantages. Such important protections as sick leave with pay, vacations with pay, health care or pensions do not accrue to them.

I do not have to spell out for you the desperate plight of these "working poor." They are people who have no one to speak for them, who are dispossessed and in most cases exploited. Bear in mind that at stake are wages alone. The federal minimum wage law governs only wages, while union workers bargain for better working conditions and additional benefits to help make life a little more secure, a little more acceptable. Although minimum-wage workers are not union members, we of the labor movement are, in effect, their representatives since we are the only voice in the United States speaking and lobbying on their behalf.

There is yet another subgroup among the unorganized "have-nots" in the U.S. labor force, rarely discussed because so little is known about them. This bottom group does not earn even the legal minimum of $2.90 per hour [1980: $3.10]. In their desperate flight to a better life here, they have entered our country improperly and are called "illegal aliens." I prefer the term "undocumented workers." No one knows how large this group is: Estimates range upwards of eight million. They are our own Third World inside the United States, taking any job at subhuman wages. Ever-cringing, never overtly complaining, always fearing deportation, they fill the new sweat shops.

Until these distinctions within the organized and unorganized labor force are understood, plans for the 1980s cannot be made wisely, and events in the labor sector may come as an unwelcome shock.

B.
Our Two-Tier Employers

Executive Program in Business Administration,
Columbia University at Arden House, Harriman, N.Y., June 6, 1979.

Everything, just everything, depends on which jobs Lady Luck makes available to you. In the job lottery, good luck is a union paper mill in your town where you can earn about $8 an hour on the average. You will work overtime, if you wish. You will have sick leave and vacations and many other benefits.

Bad luck is a hosiery mill, the only industry in town. You enter it with high hopes, but you find only seasonal work so you will average less than $4 an hour. In a union hosiery mill you earn less than half the pay of a paper mill worker and perhaps half the benefits. If you have been so spectacularly unlucky as to be caught in a non-union hosiery shop, you may earn even less per hour, perhaps only a bit more than a third of the paper mill workers, and actually below the official poverty line if you are supporting a family of four.

It occurs to you as you work that the skills you need in a hosiery or garment factory are not less than those required in a paper mill. You are paid less not because you are less able but because you have had the misfortune to work in a lower-paying industry. If you were in a higher-paying industry, you could be as inexperienced, but you would be paid better from the start. It's like the difference between the earnings of a hairdresser in a poor neighborhood and one at the town's exclusive hotel. The skills are the same, the take-home pay is not.

Why do some industries pay more than others? How does it happen that some unions can do better for their workers than others? The U.S.'s two-tier labor force is the result of the U.S.'s two-tier economy. The top tier includes the glamorous, famous brand name corporations: Mobil and Exxon, Ford and General Motors, du Pont and Monsanto, Firestone and Goodyear, IBM, Kodak, Xerox. The bottom tier are, with certain outrageous exceptions, comparatively small firms, such as local retail stores, restaurants, marginal manufacturing shops.

In 1976 all the establishments with more than 50 employees numbered less than 5 percent of all businesses. The bottom tier are legion and employ 55 percent of workers now in the private sector. Thus a majority of U.S. workers are employed by bottom tier employers, who not only pay far less for comparable skills, but often offer a shaky future to their workers. While more than 400,000 new businesses usually start up in confidence each year, a slightly smaller number go out of business the same year. Only one out of three or four new firms lasted five years in the halcyon days after World War II. Much of this is due to cutthroat competition amongst these small entrepreneurs. The U.S. labor movement would support even more free, democratic, competitive capitalism, but we insist that the raw excesses of this competition must not fall heavily upon those who have the least.

Top-tier firms who tend to have some control over their markets have ready access to lower-interest loans for high technology. They can plan years ahead and can spend millions on research and development, which helps to make their workers more productive. Behind each worker there is likely to be $40,000 or even $70,000 worth of assets. When these workers gain a little higher wage, their firms attempt to respond by investing in more efficient methods, thus achieving higher productivity. Since labor is a very much smaller portion of their cost than it is in labor-intensive industries, wage increases need not add much to the price of their goods. Unfortunately, in practice, their prices often rise dramatically.

Corporations doing $5 million or more a year in sales represent only 2½ percent of the total number of corporations but in 1974 accounted for 77 percent of sales and 87 percent of net profits before taxes.

Point for point, the bottom economy is in complete contrast. These firms cannot control any factor in their market; their markets control them entirely. They are fiercely competitive with others who make the same products. They have little working capital, little access to low-cost money, no research and development to help them become more efficient. A huge apparel factory, itself a rarity, may have $15,000 worth of assets per worker, but the typical garment shop employs 50 production workers, has perhaps $6000 net worth per worker and earns after-tax profits on sales of 1 to 2 percent in good times. The top 500 industrial corporations had 4.6 percent profit on sales in 1978 and a return on investment of 13.5 percent.

The lower-tier firms have been called the very model of free, competitive capitalism. They need to try for every advantage, and since the easiest of these is to pay workers less, they are the employers most likely to exploit labor.

These facts provide the clues that explain why the bottom group of struggling firms pay the lowest wages, so low that a responsible person can be gainfully employed but will still be below the poverty line—poor.

C.
Our Working Poor: We Must Do Better

Suppose it were in your power to wipe out poverty in the United States. How would you do it? Where would you start?

Most people would think first of putting all unemployed persons to work. But even if every unemployed person in the nation were employed, at present wage rates this would not wipe out the stain of poverty. The unemployed are only part of the people and households that suffer "economic hardship." "Economic hardship" describes the group in the labor force that includes not only the unemployed, but also the underemployed and those earning low wages. It excludes certain unemployed groups like full-time students and individuals who have the good fortune to be in families whose incomes are plentiful enough to provide protection from hardship.

Within the bottom tier of our country's two-tier labor force you will find our *working poor*. In 1974, more than 9,500,000 people were suffering economic hardship, but only 4,755,000 of these were unemployed. Thus about one-half of the people with inadequate employment and earnings were actually working, but still suffering hardship. The proportions change from year to year, yet it remains true that low pay is a main cause a person is poor; in some years low pay is the principal cause.

The government's official unemployment figures, released monthly, are important, but they do not tell us as much as we generally believe. Things are much worse in the United States than our unemployment statistics suggest. If we had, in addition, reliable, regularly-released figures that described our working poor, we would be continuously aware of the real dimensions of our problem.

We must act to eradicate poverty in the United States, to improve the living standards of all the people, not only the favored few. Full employment must be accomplished, and livable wages must be the goal. Those with the least must be provided for.

To begin with, we should have strong inheritance laws, not for people who have worked all their lives, earning $15,000 a year, or even $150,000, but for the super-rich. Great wealth must not be transmitted because this is one of the fiercest deterrents to free, democratic, competitive capitalism—populist capitalism. The children of the very rich start off too rich. The control of the means of production is passed from one generation to another without regard to merit or ability. Capitalism to be both successful and democratic must have diverse ownership and competent management, not narrow ownership and inherited management. As many people as possible must share the risks and reap the rewards of our economic system.

When great fortunes are transmitted from one generation to another, that in itself makes it almost impossible to move in the direction of a fair and rational redistribution of wealth. When these huge fortunes are kept outside the reach of government, of the people, then fewer dollars are available for the common good, particularly for those who fall out of the race.

For those with the least, a federal incomes policy based on a living minimum wage would go a long way towards alleviating poverty were it joined to a national commitment to provide employment for every person ready, willing and able to work.

Workers on the present minimum wage do not get adequate protection from their employers; they lack paid sick leave, paid vacations, paid health fees—benefits now earned by those workers who receive the average industrial wage. Taxpayers today augment the wages of the working poor with social help like Medicaid, food stamps and welfare supplements because their employers pay them so little. Therefore, I recommend that the minimum wage be pegged at 66 percent of the average industrial wage to make up the deficit, instead of the current 45 percent.

A negative income tax to provide a decent life for those who are suffering hardship is one of the ideas being put forward that deserve discussion and debate. The Full Employment Act of 1946 and the Humphrey-Hawkins Bill of 1979 together offer the underpinning of a public policy which, fleshed out, could provide the basis for an onslaught against poverty.

Providing opportunities for people to work might require sponsoring additional education, government jobs as a last resort and, above all, funds targeted to specific conditions, like unemployed black youth. Day-care centers would permit single parents with minor children to work.

Full employment at living wages benefits everyone. A lot more coats and bicycles and cars would be bought by the formerly very poor, along with other consumer goods, thereby putting many more workers to work.

I sometimes daydream that in my lifetime I will see the day when affluent Americans understand that their own self-interest, the strengthening of their money if not their morality, lies in wiping out poverty once and for all time throughout the nation.

D.
Collective Bargaining Issues In The 1980s

Executive Program at Business Administration, Columbia University at Arden House, June 6, 1979.

> The men and women in Columbia University's six-week Executive Program in Business Administration, sent by their organizations, are from the ranks of upper and middle managers from U.S. corporations as well as those from other countries.

The collective bargaining issues for the 1980s will not be the same for all unions because all unions do not confront the same problems or the same inequities. There is more than one labor movement and, though it may seem an oversimplification, it is nonetheless useful to divide our organized movement into two parts, the "haves" and the "have-nots."

Because these two tiers are so different, the aspirations of their members will generate different expectations at the bargaining table. Those in the first tier will want to assure their wages are not eroded by inflation, but they will think primarily of benefits and how to improve and expand them. In some cases I think they are going to be limited in their aspirations only by the creative intelligence of their leaders or their own imagination. As members of a group merging into the middle class, they are now interested in tax avoidance, so they will opt for benefits such as untaxable supplementary unemployment compensation.

One basic area the top tier want to move into, assuming no federal action is taken on health security, is the establishment of Health Maintenance Organizations, HMOs. Some segments of the automobile union and industry have provided that essential benefit to their workers. They will also be talking about prepaid legal fees; some workers of the United Auto Workers, the Meat Cutters and the International Brotherhood of Electrical Workers have already embarked on that experiment.

I can foretell that during the 1980s, some big, well-disciplined, militantly-led, mass-based union is going to talk to its employers about housing assistance for its workers. The kind of housing that workers can afford to buy and maintain hardly exists now and when it does, the cost of borrowing the money for it is beyond reach. With inflation going forward a number of years and mortgage rates moving into the double digit range, there is no question in my mind but that some of the major unions are going to bargain for housing assistance in the financial market unavailable to others. Employers could sponsor cooperative housing or be helpful in arranging low-cost mortgages, as an additional benefit.

Before long there will be greater emphasis on shorter hours. In 1977 the United Auto Workers made excellent progress toward the goal of a four-day week when, in the renegotiation of their agreements, they accepted a new total of 22 days off with pay, exclusive of paid vacation and sick leave.

Shorter hours will, I think, be very high on the agenda of many unions. One of the reasons is that productivity increases carry with them the risk of technological unemployment. Fewer workers are needed for automated machines so the available work must be shared. We are the most efficient work force in the world, with the highest productivity and we must raise our productivity still higher while at the same time we take great care to treat the work force in a more decent and just manner. Technological unemployment should not cause workers to lift up their hammers and attack machines. Instead, technology gives us the opportunity to reduce the eight-hour day to seven hours and thus avoid the displacement of workers. One way or another, workers will seek to protect their jobs by sharing work.

I believe there is also going to be a greater emphasis on job enrichment, making the job more satisfying, less boring. It has started in very small ways in a few places. These efforts have had little impact so far, but I believe workers are going to become more concerned about the quality of their jobs and whether they are monotonous or demeaning. Employers will be asked to put their heads together with their employees to find ways to recreate a sense of craft on the job.

I think there will be a push to add to the attractiveness of the work place as well. Negotiations might involve the rest areas of the plant, the shower and locker rooms, the athletic or recreation facilities. We may enter a period when neither union nor management feels threatened by the other, when workers are acknowledged as making a contribution and consulted about certain things, when management stops believing its authority is being eroded by the inclusion of the "natural enemy" in mutually beneficial discussions. If so, then more of the worker's life may center around the workplace and the recreational activities adjacent to the shop.

Although there are certain jobs that, it would seem to me, are almost impossible to make more attractive, no industrial jobs should be unsafe or unhealthy. There will be a major push, I believe, for employers to provide health and safety training, better monitoring and safety equipment. All the problems with life-threatening chemicals and radioactive substances must be dealt with by both workers and management working out solutions together.

Plant Relocation and Corporate Responsibility

Another very vital item that union officers and union committees are going to be concerned with is job security. Up to now unions have talked about job security in terms of seniority clauses, requiring that those who are in jobs first get the best opportunities to stay there. When a layoff occurs or some difficulty arises, new workers, who are the last ones to be hired, are the first ones to go. This principle has been fairly well established in basic labor agreements throughout the country. I am talking about a very different kind of job security. I am talking about problems caused by plant relocation. I am talking about unions wanting to have a great deal more to say about the freedom of companies to close down plants and move them elsewhere. There is no way today that anyone can say to a plant manager or owner of a corporation, "You cannot close down and move out." But in the future I think that American trade unions will be developing some formulas that may be used in the collective bargaining process to limit the right of an employer to close a factory.

Corporations, large or small, are in some respects quasi-public institutions. When one leaves, the town may collapse; a whole county may go under. The other citizens in that town, that county, must pick up the bills generated in the ensuing havoc: unemployment compensation, mortgage foreclosures, business bankruptcies, often the entire community in great distress—everyone from dentists to auto dealers, bankers to tailors. We can and must manage these traumas better.

Because they plan ahead, large firms know years in advance when they will close plants. They must give communities where such plants are located the same lead time to plan. If we are going to be genuinely concerned about the effects upon communities and working people of private decisions made for private purposes, then something will have to be done outside of collctive bargaining. Some of us will have to ask for federal regulations. Today, the Environmental Protection Agency demands impact statements when a corporation wants to change the natural shape of the landscape or put up a nuclear plant. Maybe we ought to require community impact statements before an employer can seriously consider closing a plant, with resulting unemployment and irreparable damage to the community and its residents.

Collective Bargaining in the Second Tier

Workers outside the first tier are in a very different position from the workers I have been describing. I do not know what will be the aspirations of the five million or so who depend on the national minimum wage—except to get out from under. If they think about their condition a little, if we in labor can reach out to them, they will want to join those of us who have something to say about our wages and working conditions.

The "have-nots" within labor unions, the millions who are in the lowest 20th or 25th percentile of industrial wages in this country, will reach in the coming decade for more of the usual rewards of the collective bargaining process: better wages, working conditions and benefits. I think there will be not only a drive for higher wages but also for greater equity between this group and other working groups in the country. There will be, in addition, a tremendous push to improve their sense of security about life after they stop working.

As many as two-thirds of the establishments in the United States that employ workers provide retirement plans over and above Social Security. But among the "have-nots" only a minority have even minimal retirement plans. In this period of destructive inflation, these union workers are starting to understand that they will be ground down unless their future is protected. They are becoming terribly, terribly concerned about what will happen to them when their working days are over, since they depend upon their own resources alone.

Clearly, the government has tried to combat this fear of the nation's workers by adjusting Social Security benefits in line with the increased prices consumers have to meet. But this provision has become extraordinarily costly since it is financed by employers and workers only. We have to ask ourselves whether the current working force will be able to bear the burden. The present Washington administration has already proposed trimming down Social Security benefits, in spite of the fact that the contributions are now at their highest level. If Social Security payments do not keep up with inflation, you will find those of us in unions earning within the lowest one-fourth of industrial wages wanting either to improve greatly our existing retirement programs or to start plans where there are none.

Health coverage is still not widespread among "have-not" workers. While the majority of the organized labor force has some medical insurance, "Cadillac coverage"—the important family coverage—exists by and large only in the major industries. Without a federal program, those of us in labor-intensive industries will be driving hard for family health coverage, for dental and eye care, for drug prescription plans.

Women's Issues

With more and more women in the work force and with more and more of them in jobs traditionally considered men's hallowed preserves—mining, construction, steel, auto manufacturing—employers are already confronted with a whole new list of demands. Labor-intensive industries have had women workers for generations and have not yet addressed their needs. These demands may be won first in capital-intensive industries through collective bargaining. We have paid maternity leave for some women workers: this should be made universal. Flexible working hours, flex-time, and shared-time jobs are other important needs. You can count on these being on the agenda in some areas.

A serious problem women confront is job classification. We have been paying lip service for a long time to the slogan, "Equal pay for equal worth." Some U.S. employers have done more than just give this lip service, but certainly not all. Too many still fail to do so. Now women are beginning to introduce a new concept: "Comparable pay for comparable worth".

If a steel worker must work nine and one-half hours, what should a data-processing operator be paid for the same time period? You cannot compare the two jobs, but you can discuss comparable worth. Should a woman sewing-machine operator, who needs skill and coordination to do her job, be paid as much as or more than someone working for General Electric who is only a machine watcher? At GE, the machine does the job; the worker's responsibility is to watch the sparkle of lights and, when they all go red at the same time, to call someone to come and fix the mechanism. This problem of comparable worth is an enlargement of the "equal pay for equal work" concept. It will become a collective bargaining issue, but may require some federal interposition.

Federal Legislation

Women have been asking for years, "How about day-care centers?" All the children of our nation must be brought up well for they are our future; working parents must have safe, low-cost places for their youngsters. This essential requirement will produce a drive for the federal government to subsidize day-care centers throughout the country.

Day-care centers are an example of a worker need that cannot be obtained through collective bargaining but must be provided by the federal government. Another such need is a standard Unemployment Compensation Act to replace the anarchy of the current system: 52 different laws for the 50 states, the District of Columbia and Puerto Rico in addition to the Federal Unemployment Tax Act. We desperately need a uniform, humane law to ease the terrible effect of joblessness on workers and their families.

We will also have to turn to the government for ways to narrow the chasm between those at the lowest wage levels and those at the highest. Collective bargaining cannot help very much here. Individual employers, no matter how generous they may be, are unable to correct this condition.

There is no secret about how the oil workers, steel workers, rubber workers, transportation workers, and the public service workers got to where they are. They work for enterprises that are monopolies or share a monopoly or have such strong market positions that they call the tune for their industries. The rest of us deal in the other economy of small employers who are undercapitalized and have little or no market position. In my own garment industry, the overwhelming number of employers are among the last genuine capitalists in the United States—they truly participate in a system of free, democratic, competitive capitalism. Tens of thousands of these employers are at each other's throats for a share of the market and they often seek an advantage by exploiting their workers. Workers in such highly competitive, labor-intensive industries are going to be looking to government regulation and government interposition. For when we talk of protecting ourselves, where else shall we seek help?

We can look only to the federal government to help narrow the gap between those who have and those who have not. We need more egalitarianism in the workforce and greater opportunity for workers to live decently and with dignity, whether or not they are union members. A higher minimum wage will help to achieve this goal, as would an incomes policy. If it is true that we are moving into an inflationary cycle of some three to six years, then perhaps we must devise an incomes policy to keep wages in the topmost tier from zooming while wages in the bottommost tier cannot keep up with the cost of living.

Real health security also requires federal action. A Health Care Act would be a godsend to all the workers in this country, which is why union leaders and members are so eager to support such legislation. Too great a share of our economy is ripped out by medical costs. We are the last industrial country where health care is not provided across the board. Federal action is long overdue.

Finally, the 1980s may also see a push for an "hours" bill. As industries automate to become more productive, there will be less work but many more workers. If it is not possible for even the giant unions to negotiate a shorter work week through collective bargaining, then we can expect to see a tremendous effort made in Congress for the establishment of a shorter work day in order to share the remaining work and thus eliminate the unemployment caused by high technology.

Return to the Rhetoric of the 1930s?

I would leave you on a cautionary note. I think the 1980s will be a challenging time. We in the labor movement will have to beat back the challenge of many employers who seem to want a return of the class struggle. This country has not suffered from this attitude for 40 years. In the 1930s when many industries were being organized, forming a union was stark; the struggle was bitter. Workers had to join together to fight against the employer who exploited and oppressed them and against the community which the employer controlled.

We thought that kind of confrontation had been done away with, put to rest. We thought we no longer needed to expend a great deal of our energy in that direction. We thought the rhetoric of the 1930s and the 1940s was a dead language. Yet that rhetoric has been resurrected by some employers, by the National Association of Manufacturers, by something called the "Committee for a Union-Free Environment."

Very few union leaders are being fooled. If we are to be challenged on the job, in mines, mills and factories, then we too shall revert to the old rhetoric and start with, "Don't let the bastards take it away!"

"Union-free environment" is a new slogan that sets a certain tone. It establishes a standard to which some Stone Age employers may wish to repair. If employers do gather round this slogan, there will be many difficult days ahead for both workers and management. I would not suggest using a renewed class struggle as the basis for contemplating the future. I would hope we do not come to that. But if we do, then all bets are off so far as rational, equitable collective bargaining is concerned.

My own hope is that we will seek out the best thinking of the best thinkers among our friends from government and academia, as well as in the U.S. labor movement. Ray Marshall, Secretary of Labor, has been a most effective advocate of the interplay of those disparate elements that play a major role in evolving labor-management policy: By communicating with each other, they can bring into reasonable balance the apparent conflicts among the objectives each group seeks for itself.

We need to encourage everyone to think about these problems. Together we will discard programs that may no longer be useful and concentrate on existing programs we ought to improve or on new ones that might be suggested. I prefer to believe that labor and management will join together to point the way to a freer, more equitable, more secure United States.

"UNION LABEL"

Words: PAULA GREEN
Music: MALCOLM DODDS

Look for the un-ion lab-el when you are buy-ing a coat, dress or blouse. Re-mem-ber some-where our un-ion's sew-ing our wage-s go-ing to feed the kids and run the house, we work hard but who's com-plain-ing. Thanks to the I. L. G. we're pay-ing our way. So, al-ways look for the un-ion la-bel, it says we're a-ble to make it in the U. S. A.

four

The Constant Struggle

A.

"Always Look For The Union Label"

**International Labor Press Association, ILPA,
Los Angeles, California, December, 1977.**

> In November, 1975, the ILGWU started a unique TV and radio campaign, complete with catchy jingle, to educate consumers. During the 1977 AFL-CIO convention, Leon Stein, former editor of *Justice* and a founder of ILPA, asked Chaikin to tell about it since this was the first time any union had bought national air time as part of a sustained program.

From a high of 457,517 members in 1969, membership in the ILG fell more than 26,000 by 1973, due to increasing imports. It plummeted 30,000 more by 1975. Thirty years of hard-fought gains had been lost in two years because of political decisions made in Washington after the oil embargo of 1973. We were just coming out of a terrible recession. Morale amongst the workers and members of the staff was low; employer groups, too, were not feeling optimistic. In addition, we were planning to send 110 new organizers out into the field and were concerned that they would meet with a wary, uninformed population who would be unsympathetic to organizers eager to convey a union message. Clearly many people did not know the ILG or what it stands for.

Our ILG union label had been around for many, many years. People were saying it was old hat and ineffective. It needed rejuvenation and I was convinced that a combination of TV, radio, newspaper and bus ads, as outlined by our very creative advertiser, Paula Green, would give our people a terrific boost.

We designed the program to meet a number of goals. At the top of the list was the need to increase the name recognition of the union, which was not too widely known outside the New York area. Perhaps we could redesign the union label, upgrade its quality and place it where it would be readily seen. Workers had to be motivated to sew the label in, to understand it could make a difference.

Equally important was our need to go to the President and Congress to seek help in order to cope with our import problem. We wanted them to be impressed by a union which had the will and the resources to make this a public issue. Moreover, 24 Senators and many more Congressmen came from states and districts with no ILG members. In my view, our best chance to educate their constituencies was through statements coming at them from TV and radio. We hoped our message would create understanding of the need to keep U.S. men and women working, and empathy for the problems caused by unregulated imports.

We began with a 60-second spot—twice the usual length for greatest impact. The ad campaign featured the catchy jingle, "Always Look for the Union Label," sung by ILGers themselves in both English and Spanish. It appeared first on the *Flip Wilson TV Special* of November 11, 1975 and then on TV specials like *Roots*, the *Academy Awards* and *60 Minutes*. The song took hold from the start. Johnny Carson sang it, Merv Griffin featured it, Carol Burnett parodied it, song books included it. Paula Green's lyrics end with a play on words, "Look for the Union Label...it says we're able to make it in the

U.S.A." This was our double message—the label proves the garment was made in the United States and because it was, union members are able to make a living. The ILG had a hit!

We plastered subways and buses with long signs that read "Nothing suits us like our union suits." Displays in the labor press reminded other trade union members, "If union families don't look for the union label, who will?" During the bicentennial we added a felicitous line: "Think of it as a little American flag in your clothes." The campaign has been seen in

Nothing suits us like our union suits. Jeepers! Creepers from the International Ladies' Garment Workers' Union. Stitch, stitch, hooray! Made in U.S.A.

the black press, the fashion press, leading newspapers and magazines around the nation.

Over the years our very versatile executive vice-president Wilbur Daniels has been responsible for this extensive campaign and guided it through its early moments to its established success. The cost of this media blitz was $2.1 million for each of the first two years [and another $4½ million through 1979]. Hardly the $360 million of Proctor and Gamble's annual ad budget but still a lot of money for working people.

Toward the end of 1976, we wanted to find out whether our media drive was reaching the public. Surveys taken by a market research organization concluded that the ads were effective. People in all walks of life were more aware of the ILG and its label and said that they were also "more likely to buy union-made clothes." They tended to view the International Ladies' Garment Workers' Union as acting in the public interest. The message was coming through. Senators and Congresspeople stopped Evelyn Dubrow, our international vice-president and Washington legislative director, in the halls of Congress to sing her the union label song. More than that, they were beginning to listen to her exhortations that a rational trade policy is essential in order to maintain our country's strong manufacturing base.

B.

"Right To Work" Or "Right To Work For Less"?

Presidential Classroom for Young Americans, Washington, D.C., February 8, 1980.

Each year 300 to 400 top U.S. high school students take part in a week-long seminar on the relationships among government, business and labor. After Chaikin's talk, the first student asked a question about the legitimacy of union shops. Right to Work laws, which make it possible for a person to work in a union shop without joining the union, operate in 22 states.

QUESTION: Why should a worker have to pay tribute in the form of union dues in order to keep his job?

CHAIKIN: The National Labor Relations Act provided an orderly means whereby workers could become members of a union of their own choosing, a union that the majority of the workers elects as the bargaining agent for all the workers in that unit.

This simply means that when the union negotiates a collective agreement with an employer providing higher wages, benefits, job security and many other protections, the worker who was indifferent or in opposition is the beneficiary of the agreement equally with those who supported the union.

The union, whose responsibility it is to enforce the agreement, is a permanent organization the year round, with operating costs to meet like salaries, rent, electricity and other normal administration expenses. It is only fair that all of the workers covered by the agreement should share the burdens equitably since they share the benefits.

In the United States there is a well-established principle that individuals cannot on their own decide whether or not they should contribute taxes necessary to support the common good.

Whether they wish to refrain for one reason or another from contributing their fair share is not their choice. For example, even when families have no children at school, if they own property they are still required to support the school system.

There is nothing alien, unacceptable or unfair in the theory that all should share equally in the support of an activity the majority has agreed upon.

Most Americans are not free loaders. They prefer to pull their own weight. Where there is little or no pressure against joining the union, there is very little difficulty in a union's maintaining a very substantial membership. At first the Taft-Hartley Act required that workers must vote positively in order to give union negotiators the right to seek a union shop clause. There was enormous grass roots support! In most cases 95 to 100 percent were in favor of these union shop agreements. Senator Taft, after whom the law was named, was so embarrassed by this groundswell of union support that he moved at the next Congressional session to throw out the requirement from the law, and most of his fellow Republicans rushed to vote with him.

> QUESTION: Would the death of Right to Work laws automatically mean that workers would be readily organized?

CHAIKIN: No, absolutely not. Right to Work legislation hampers the union in its effort to represent workers only *after* they have formed into a union and *after* the union agreement has been bargained out and enforced.

In organizing new plants, the union will confront the same problems it always does. It will still have to overcome the fear that workers have of management and retaliation, threats and coercion often leveled against workers seeking to form unions.

Right to Work legislation is viewed as an expression of the public policy of the state, and thus it adds greatly to the anti-union attitudes which may exist in greater or lesser degree from county to county. From that point of view, the abolition of Right to Work legislation may help to create a fair climate in which union organization may take place as granted by law.

C.

Industrial Citizen: Organizing The Unorganized

To various union boards and locals from 1973 to 1979.

The ILGWU moves on many fronts to educate senators, representatives, presidents, opinion leaders of all kinds, and the general public. But the most important task of any union is winning new members and organizing new shops. Organizing the garment industry, however, is unlike union activity in other places. When a new steel plant or auto plant is opened in some far-off spot, it is considered by its steel or auto union to be a child of the mother company, all of whose off-spring are to be union shops automatically. The mother company does not necessarily take the same view, but unionizing the new facility is always a matter for discussion, debate and collective bargaining.

The garment industry has few such sprawling companies to bargain with collectively. Only 10 Master Agreements were written in 1979, covering 21,600 workers, barely four percent of the total membership. Most new apparel factories spring up in outlying districts like orphans, not affiliated with a conglomerate, each one needing individual tending and education before it joins the union family.

Chaikin speaks about organizing the unorganized in nearly every speech he gives to a union audience.

We Must Do More Than Seek a Better Life For Ourselves

Let me talk with you and share some of the problems we confront as this decade closes. The first problem is organizing the unorganized. Despite all the union institutions, despite all the fancy pants speeches, the arguments, discussions and activities we engage in, the one single most important responsibility that the union has is to organize the unorganized.

Why do we do it? We do it to help protect the standards we have erected over the years. No matter how poor union wages and union conditions are, you know that union is much better than non-union. If you are uncertain, let me remind you.

Wage costs consist of two major parts. One is the wage that is put into the pay envelopes and the other is the value of the worker benefits. These are usually called fringe benefits, but there is nothing fringe about them. When you go to a non-union shop you sometimes meet people who earn almost as much as union workers do. You ask them, "How much do you make?" After they tell you they add, "That's almost like union wages." Sometimes it is union wages, but what they neglect to tell you is that they have no pension and few if any holidays with pay, and they do not get two, three or four weeks vacation with pay. There is no Blue Cross, Blue Shield or Major Medical plan—not for themselves, much less the family coverage some of our members have. In a union shop, the value of the workers benefits on top of wages runs 26 to 28 percent, while in non-union shops it may be three to five percent. This is a major difference.

One reason to organize is to give our employers a little better break in the competitive market. A union employer cannot compete with scandalously low-paying shops here in the United States, let alone the almost no-wage shops in most foreign countries. We understand that garment manufacturing is almost the last industry in this country made up of small units competing meanly with each other for the consumers' hard-earned dollar. There are only so many pennies and dollars that each family has, and every family divides up its dollars the way it wants to spend them—for food, for housing, for entertainment and something for clothes. But worse than the general competition for the public's dollars are the tens of thousands of individual employers competing against each other for just those clothing dollars.

In most large industries, workers are all in unions. When you have non-union labor competing against union labor, as we do in garment manufacturing, things are much more difficult. The non-union part of the industry undercuts everyone, increasing the jungle competition. Add imports made by low-wage workers and you have the final straw for many of our employers.

These are not the only reasons we organize. If we lived for ourselves alone, people would recognize us as a good and decent organization. Yet we must do more than seek a better life for just ourselves. We owe to non-union workers the opportunity to organize to help themselves. We owe it to them as human beings; we owe it to them as fellow citizens. If we think we know a better way, we have an obligation to make that better way available to them. But social unionism is an idea they have to understand, an idea they have to accept. This is something they must live. People who think about a union and who understand and accept it become the kind of members and leaders whom we want.

So we begin with becoming an industrial citizen, with the idea of union, the idea that we have a duty to help each other live just a little better tomorrow than we live today.

The New Sweatshops

When we talk about organizing the unorganized, we're back 80 years to the beginning of the century, to the time of the great immigrations. Today in many areas of greater New York, lower California and the Southwest, we have the same situation once more: people coming to seek opportunity in this great country. They believe that, no matter how badly they are treated here, no matter how desperately they have to work to make a living, life is better here than what they left behind. You know that is true because people vote with their feet. They leave their homes in Mexico, South America, the Caribbean, Vietnam. They take desperate chances to get here. Their journeys are filled with danger. They come without money, without resources, without friends, and they come illegally. It's plain how desperate their drive is to find a better life. They come, work in new sweatshops for very little, and they live and toil in fear that somebody will turn them in and send them back.

That's one of the greatest challenges we face today. I do

not have to exaggerate it, but I do not want to minimize it either. You know the sweatshops are growing and you know the regions in which they are growing. You know how desperately they threaten the established union shops. You can see them in the same neighborhood, around the corner, sometimes in the same building.

I think we can organize them. I think so not because I am a mystic, not because I read it in the stars, but because we in the ILGWU have organized these hell-holes before. In the early 1900s they were as vicious, as depressing, as de-humanizing, but even more widespread. Many of the people who worked in those sweatshops were also in this country illegally. But, in time, we organized them.

People are very little different today. They may look a little different, speak a different language, come with different cultures, but they are human beings like we are and, what is as important, they are workers who have a community of interest with us. Somehow we must find the key to unlock their hopes, allay their fears. They need to understand that when we talk to them, we do not talk as police officers or immigration officials. We talk as workers. That is the challenge and we must pursue it.

You and I are Born of a Common Mother: Exploitation.

Let me talk with you simply as an organizer who has spent the better part of his life trying to organize garment workers in Maine, New Hampshire and Vermont, in Massachusetts, New Jersey, Pennsylvania and Maryland, in Texas, Oklahoma, Arkansas and Louisiana, and just a few states in between.

Let me, on behalf of the tens of thousands of garment workers living and working hundreds and hundreds of miles from New York City, bring thanks to you for your help and your support.

They do not know your faces, they hardly know of your existence or your own problems, but they know you gave money to them for flood relief, gave money to support organizers in the field and to pay their expenses from town to town under some of the worst possible obstacles.

They know you helped them fight hard-bitten southern reactionaries. They were up against unscrupulous employers who held whole communities in the palms of their hands, trying to stave off the organization of garment workers who earned so little. When I worked with them as an organizer, we shared the same hopes and the same fears, the same struggles and the occasional little successes. These workers did not know you, but they knew that without your help they would have little future in the shops.

I bring you their thanks, and I call you brother and sister. I call you brother and sister even though you may be of different ethnic background from myself, of different color or different religion. I call you brother and sister because you and I are born of a common mother—exploitation. We found exploitation in the 1900s, the 1920s and just yesterday.

Only Through Your Sacrifice Can the Unorganized Be Organized

Today your sacrifices continue to make a difference. Through your dues you support your local and the International headquarters. We in turn seek out young people willing to make the necessary commitment and sacrifice working as organizers in communities where unions are hated, where workers are fearful that if the boss discovers they talked to a union organizer, they will lose their jobs.

I am not going to repeat the ugly stories of the southern states, of how the people who control the politics of those states smash the union movement wherever they find it, of the Right to Work laws in those states which sound like they promise the right to a job, but really mean the Right to Work for Less, the Right to Low Wages.

I won't go into detail about the heroism of individual organizers who, at the risk of their lives even today, try to organize workers in the factories of our southern states. But I will say that the competition that comes from those non-union shops, and the occasional competition that comes from non-union shops here around New York, is bitter and ugly to live with.

In their search for cheap labor, our employers have found it expedient to move out of New York all across the country, and then out of the country altogether to the sweatshops of Korea, the Philippines and elsewhere. Employers in this industry are not much different from employers elsewhere. They are in business not as a social welfare activity. Their credo is not the greatest good for the greatest number. They are in business for profit and occasionally, in their pervasive pursuit of profit, they lose sight of human values. They care more about getting their work done for the cheapest possible price than about the operator who has worked long, arduously and loyally and who needs that pay for her family's needs. If anyone will work for 16 cents an hour in some exotic country, so much the better for profits.

Picketing: Chaikin and Wilbur Daniels; ILGWU executive vice-president.

Have we reason to be optimistic today? From 1900, when this union was started, to the place where we find ourselves today, can we be tremendously optimistic?

It's a difficult thing to wait in a shop, frustrated. But there is no choice for any of us. Without the union to help us fight, this entire system would collapse. The fight will be difficult but there is no alternative for us. Not we in the International union headquarters nor you in the locals will be permitted to sit back and let events continue. If we do not have the methods now, if we do not have the smarts now, then we are going to have to find new ways to do it, new approaches, new wisdom.

D.

Political Citizen: Politics Is Everybody's Business

**Political Rally, Local 295,
Pittston, Pa., October 19, 1972.**

The challenge of the coming decade is one we must face both as citizens of this great country and as members of this great union.

Most of us are Americans, most of us are eligible to vote. We were either born here or we became citizens. It's fine to be a citizen. But if you do not use your citizenship, it is a waste. Like a muscle you must use, your citizenship needs exercising or it has no strength, no purpose. When you exercise the rights that are derived from it, you can make something worthwhile for yourselves and your families, for your friends and your neighbors as well.

When you vote, you are political citizens, and when you joined this union you became industrial citizens. Being an industrial citizen in the United States means that you have decided to have something to say as an individual worker employed by employers large or small, strong or weak. You have decided you have something to say about the value of your time in the shop. We have come a long way from the days when working people had nothing to say about their day-to-day lives and nothing to say about their destinies. We came this great distance as the result of many common endeavors, in union. No worker came that long way from exploitation because of what he or she did alone. We have arrived at this point because we held our hands out to each other, in union. The strong held out their hands to the weak, the people with courage held out their hands to the fearful, the wiser ones held out their hands to the slower ones, those who could speak out and yell held their hands out to those too shy and timid to represent themselves. Now we are industrial citizens, joined together in union, and we face tremendous challenges.

Think about the events in Washington today. We have pressing business that needs doing. We want to do something about the high price of food, about a health plan for everyone, about a new minimum wage to give millions a chance to live decently. These are all political questions.

The ILG maintains political and education departments, headed by Gus Tyler, Assistant President of the union. A brilliant writer and speaker, his is an uncanny ability to articulate the aims and objectives of the trade union movement. His departments provide the impetus for workers' education within the union and the necessity for tying aspects of our program to the political candidates who would advance it.

Now at election time, we remind you to become political citizens. We have been taught the bitter lesson that what we have won on the picket line and in collective bargaining is often lost when an unfriendly administration comes along. If there are people here who wonder why we talk politics at a union meeting, let them stop wondering. Politics is everybody's business and particularly the business of our union members.

The ILGWU Garment Workers Rally—1976.

E.
Our Own Third World: Immigration As A Dilemma For U.S. Trade Unionists

American Immigration and Citizenship Conference,
New York, N.Y., April 9, 1976.
and the Institute of Collective Bargaining,
Automation House, New York, N.Y., November 16, 1976.

The number of immigrants permitted legally into the United States is about 400,000 a year. Most of these are the non-working family members of the 160,000 who will enter a labor force now in excess of 100 million. Some of these come in under special refugee acts, but most are permitted entry only because they have a job, guaranteed and waiting. Since their number is less than two-tenths of one percent of those employed, it is considered "insignificant" by the ILGWU and no threat to U.S. workers.

While legal immigrants pose no threat to the U.S. labor force, illegal aliens do because they are the vulnerable workers hidden inside the nation's new sweatshops. Their number is unknown and guesses vary wildly, from one to twelve million by the Immigration and Naturalization Service down to a few hundred thousand permanent ones by some researchers.

The garment industry has traditionally been a point of entry for every immigrant group into the industrial life of the United States. I can trace them from the Germans and the Irish when there was no mass production in the industry, to the Eastern European Jews in the early 1900s and the Italians who followed, to the recent immigrants of the last two decades, the blacks up from our own South, the Spanish-speaking, the Chinese, the Koreans and now the Vietnamese. The soft-goods, labor-intensive industries have been the way into a working life for all these groups.

Garment making now is not limited to the latest groups of immigrants, the blacks and Spanish-speaking. Many more white people than black are members of our union; we have about a 20 percent black membership. In Appalachia, for example, the industry was an entryway for poor whites, as it has always been for the dispossessed, for the exploited, for the inarticulate, for those not literate in the English language. You did not have to be personable, as a salesperson at Nieman Marcus was expected to be, in order to get the job. You only needed reasonable coordination and intelligence and the capacity to be trained. Human beings, with very few exceptions, are that. It was a damn tough job, but you could come in and make a beginning if you were highly motivated. Throughout our land, these jobs always went, not to those experienced, trained in tool and die making, and not to those with secretarial or computer technology skills, but to people with little or no industrial experience.

Our industry has never discriminated against anybody, regardless of race, creed, color, gender or national origin. Just the opposite. The industry has always *exploited* everybody, regardless of race, creed, color, gender, or national origin.

We in the ILG welcomed all who wanted to work as long as there was opportunity for them to do that work. Our very union was formed not only *of* immigrants but *by* immigrants. Over the years, because of this policy, we have faced expressions of disrespect, even calumny, from our fellow trade unionists, particularly at times of high unemployment, but still we raised our voices in behalf of workers coming from abroad.

We have always said that there is enough to share in this great growing democracy of ours. Freedom is indivisible and has no limits; nobody who breathes freely takes my portion from me. On the contrary, when more are free, the freer am I.

As long as the American industrial and economic community was expanding, as long as it was possible to have an optimistic view of the future, we could and would stand up for what we knew was right and proper. We expected those of us who were underemployed to become better employed, those of us who were out of work to find work. In time that work would return to our families a fair measure of economic well-being.

When, however, the U.S. community—not the U.S. working force, but the U.S. community—fails us by providing too little work, then our strong traditions appear as weak reeds. It becomes very difficult to sustain the time-honored traditions of a union that has always had a positive outlook toward the homeless, the refugees, those with the initiative to pick up stakes and come thousands of miles to a new, strange land.

Over the last several years we have been a union under siege. We are beset not only by questions from among our own members, but also urgings from other trade unionists. We have been confronted with recession and the import penetration of our markets. We have also had to cope with the millions of people in this country who have come in outside the legally established quotas. We call them undocumented workers; others call them illegal aliens. They do not enter as other newcomers do. For example, certain aliens are executives of multinational corporations sent to run or to create new industries. Undocumented aliens generally come as the dispossessed, the suppressed, the exploited. They are often illiterate, in many cases without useful work experience. Those who flow across the Mexican border into the exploiting farms of the Southwest are well known. Less known are those who come into the urban centers, in California, New York, Philadelphia, Boston, as far inland as Chicago. They follow the time-honored immigrant path to industrial jobs in the United States and find a welcome in garment factories.

We who work in labor-intensive industries such as apparel are in the front line of attack from our own members whose jobs are daily being threatened and usurped.

When aliens or other workers come into union factories, we do not ask where they come from. We do not ask their race, creed, color or national origin. We do not ask whether or not they are citizens. We ask only, "Do you want to work? Do you understand the meaning and nature of union? Will you hold your hands out to each of our other brothers and sisters in order cooperatively and collectively to raise the economic standards of all who work under the agreement that we have negotiated with employers?"

We have no difficulty with undocumented workers or illegal aliens who come into our union. They are entitled to the same rights and benefits as all other workers in the shops. These rights are derived from the existence of a collective bargaining relationship.

Some employers, on the other hand, are interested in hiring undocumented workers because they are a first line of defense against the efforts of union organizers who bring the message of a better wage and a better life. Our organizers in New York City, Philadelphia and particularly Los Angeles come to us with horror stories of the absolute, abject exploitation of workers by unscrupulous employers. When union organizers come they are shunned because undocumented workers are afraid to sign their names to union cards. They know they are in the hands of the merciless employer who can and will pick up the phone, call the Immigration Service and "turn them in." Through the barrios of these communities come the whispered admonitions to lay low, keep your head down, stay out of sight and, particularly, never sign a union card.

We can document many heartrending stories. There are times we have been able to persuade undocumented workers to sign with the union because they have rights as workers in the shop. On one occasion, in California, we had one of these groups signed up and out on strike. Courageously, they found the strength to rebel against the oppression in the shop and march in the picket line. Scabs who went through the line were also undocumented workers. The Immigration Service was called, came to raid the shop and, outrageously, approached only the picket line. Every alien picket was taken off the line and hauled into jail—but the undocumented scabs working inside the factory were not touched.

Our union put up bail money and our union lawyers appeared in court to defend these undocumented workers because our responsibility toward them was the same as our responsibility toward any American worker who signifies his or her interest in joining our union and who thereby gets into difficulty. Some officers of other unions questioned our decision; even some officers in our own International asked whether we were doing the right thing. I replied that I was not yet ready to desert the long-standing tradition which, in my judgment, had helped make the ILG great. We acted as we did because we were aware of the shameful conditions and unconscionably low wages in factories filled with aliens who are in no position to demand their rights and get for themselves ordinary, decent treatment. All this results in extraordinarily bitter economic competition between the union and non-union worker.

What do we do under these circumstances? At AFL-CIO conferences I listen to tales of agony and cries of anguish from representatives of U.S. workers who remonstrate that tens of thousands of their members have lost their jobs to undocumented workers and that the administration in Washington predicts that over 7 percent of its working force will be unemployed into the 1980s. An incredible 7 percent! In Japan and Germany, unemployment of 2 to 4 percent is enough to send their governments into high gear with remedies because they understand the consequences of unemployment.

Trade union leaders who hate any thought of surplus unemployment are besieged every day by their own members for some kind of help and when they hear that some part of their distress is due to aliens who are competitors for whatever jobs remain, the discussion becomes scathing and stinging.

I am certain that you would battle very long and very hard for your ideals, and I hope you have a measure of sympathy for approximately 7 million U.S. workers who are without jobs, whose families and children are very dear to them, who over the years have struggled to acquire some small measure of economic security and who, during this recession, have found this security swept away without any hope that their condition will improve.

Today, millions of unemployed men and women in the

United States look to the jobs they once held, only to find that if these jobs still exist, they are filled by others. God help us if we return to the days of the Know-Nothings who sought to elect only the native-born to office and to establish a 25-year residence qualification for citizenship—this was back in the 1850s when the United States had a population of only 20 million. God help us if we return to the divisiveness, the contempt and fear that reigned in the early 1920s when people who were here for only 10 or 15 years looked askance at newer arrivals. We do not want that.

You are concerned with one of humanity's most important efforts: befriending the stranger at our gates. We in the ILG want to serve your ideals as well as or better than you have been serving them. But if you want to move toward your objectives of more open immigration into this country, of opportunity for people who have the guts to come here, who have a burning desire to leave their homeland in order to improve their lives, then I think you must first demand that our society guarantee a job for every man and woman willing and able to work.

Immigration affects not only the domestic scene but also our foreign relations as well. Make no mistake about it, unless this is a United States of full employment, decent opportunity and economic security for all who are here, there will be no opportunity for undocumented workers or even legal immigrants.

As you resume your deliberations, bear in mind that you have not one goal but many. The best avenue toward reaching some of your objectives is to help and support those of us who want an expanding United States, not only a land of hope and prosperity for new immigrants, but for all of us, those who are here and those who are coming.

five

Where There Are No Free Trade Unions There Are No Other Human Rights

A.
The United States Is Not An Island

ILGWU Archives,
New York, NY, January 24, 1980.

These ILG Archives are filled with references to our concern for free democratic trade unions and social movements overseas. Our vice presidents and particularly the president always seem to have a bag packed, heading for some foreign country. These outreaches began decades ago with our president, David Dubinsky, who understood that the United States was not an island entire unto itself but that workers could display and maintain a large degree of solidarity with each other even though their hands reached thousands of miles across oceans.

Somewhere in the archives are the stories about our help to the unions of western Europe that were smashed when Hitler took control. They will describe the support the ILG gave as an organization and, above that, the dollars contributed voluntarily by members—half a day's pay, a day's pay. Remember, our members were hardly very well paid themselves.

The archives hold the record of our support for some British trade unionists, especially British seamen, when we built rest homes for them, not only in Great Britain, but also in China before it was overrun by Mao Tse-Tung. These were symbols of solidarity in our common fight against nazism and fascism.

In the archives are the accounts of our concerns for the State of Israel, 28 years before it became a nation, and our continuous support for Histadrut, the labor federation of Israel. It contains stories of our kinship with Italian workers struggling against fascism, their struggle supported by Local 89. Our interest in post-war Italy continues to this present moment with our support of CISL and UIL, the non-communist unions. We also reach out to Force Ouvriere, the non-communist French labor group.

We have a long record of helping vocational schools in France, Italy, Israel, North Africa and elsewhere. We have always been very supportive of such schools because labor is interested in training the untrained. ORT [Organization for Rehabilitation and Training] has a motto: "If you give people fish, you give them lunch. Teach them to fish and you prepare them for life."

Today, through my travels, I continue the ILG tradition of advancing the cause of free trade unionism around the world. A free trade union is a basic tenet of human rights. Where there are no free trade unions there are no other human rights.

In repressed societies like Chile or Argentina my objective

in speaking out is to lessen the terror against trade unionists and work for the release of prisoners. In somewhat freer societies like Brazil and Korea my motive is to encourage a more independent labor stance, separate from government.

When you look at the ILG today, you find us speaking to the same ends on the question of human rights as we did back in 1900 and each of the days and months and years since.

>Several ILGWU officers in addition to president Chaikin are engaged in international work.

Henoch Mendelsund, Director of the international relations department, serves as a vice-president and one of the five members of the executive committee of ITGLWF, International Textile, Garment & Leather Workers' Federation, a group of unions from some 66 countries who meet to discuss mutual problems. Since his retirement as an ILG vice-president, he has launched and is Director of the ILGWU Archives.

Shelley Appleton, secretary-treasurer, is the president of the World ORT Union. The ILGWU has supported ORT schools in Italy, Israel and France, most particularly a vocational school in Montreuil, a suburb of Paris.

Fred Siems, executive vice-president, has undertaken several goodwill missions under the auspices of the African-American Labor Council. In November 1979 he presented medical equipment to trade unions in Mali and Mauritania.

Edward Schneider, vice-president, has three international duties. He is the ILGWU representative to Western Hemisphere meetings of the North American section of the ITGLWF and participates in the activities of AIFLD, the American Institute for Free Labor Development as well as ORIT, Organizacione Regional Interamericana de Trabajadores, the Western Hemisphere section of the ICFTU, International Confederation of Free Trade Unions.

Jay Mazur, vice-president, has represented the ILGWU in Southeast Asia and South Africa.

Frank Longo, vice-president, headed a delegation visiting counterpart unions in Italy. After the 1976 flood in Italy, he disbursed monies the ILGWU had raised on behalf of destitute workers. In Mondello, Italy, the ILGWU supports the FDR Institute, a vocational training school.

B.
Exporting Democracy

**Virginia State AFL-CIO convention,
Roanoke, Va., August 22, 1974.**

When you attend the national AFL-CIO convention, you see representatives of 75 to 85 nations from different parts of the world—with different creeds, different colors, different accents, different languages. They come to our great conventions as observers to listen and learn. They listen and learn and then take back the most valuable treasure we offer them, the living idea of a free trade union movement.

We are assembled here today, each of us with a full and free opportunity to stand up, get to the mike, say what's on our minds while people listen, argue it out, vote on it and carry out the wishes of the majority. These are sure signs of great strength. These are human rights. This is what we have that we want to export to other labor movements.

Why do we do it? Because we want democracy to flourish not here alone but in the rest of the world as well. We do it because we know that if the lights of democracy are extinguished in one country after another, it is going to be much more difficult to maintain our system here, standing alone, facing a hostile and unfriendly world. We do what we can, as representatives of a free trade union movement, to encourage the idea and the practice of democracy, the establishment of human rights, not only in the older democracies, but in the newer emerging countries of the Middle East, Africa and Asia.

Democracies have been under attack almost from the end of World War II. The United Nations, which had 51 members, now has almost 151, but the leaders of too many of the new countries enslave their own peoples. Their values are not our values.

On our agenda we should place the question of our

relationship with the Soviet Union, that great, difficult, overbearing, powerful communist system. The last U.S. administration embarked on what they advertised as a detente. Everyone in this country would want to sit down and have an honest-to-God, open, comfortable relationship with the peoples of the Soviet Union. This world is one and it is too small for us to be at each other's throats. We know we can kill every Russian and they can kill every American within the space of hours. There ought to be a way to begin a dialogue, to begin to live with each other. But I contend that we have given away more than we have gained. They are enticing us to provide them with computer technology and industrial capability without lessening their system of dictatorship or their territorial aggrandizement. They are as interested today in taking over what they can as they ever were.

At the end of World War II they took over countries bordering the Soviet Union, and throughout the 1950s and 1960s they continued to prod and push. Yet the Nixon administration sold them wheat, which Americans could have used; they sold the wheat at a ridiculously low price and we Americans subsidized it through the use of our tax dollars. Did we get any lessening of the terror in their country? Did we get any possibility for dissent in their country? Did we get any hope for a real dialogue between us, social intercourse or free and unobstructed travel back and forth? No, we did not.

I submit that if we continue on that course, we are deluding ourselves about what the end result may be. Look at what has happened in the Middle East. During a time of detente, a time of theoretical good feeling, the Russian armies and air forces supplied guns, expertise, missiles, bombs and artillery of all types to Egypt, and in October, 1973, the State of Israel was once again attacked.

Why are we interested in the State of Israel? It is not just because its citizens happen to oppose some of the policies that Middle Eastern feudal sheiks have imposed on their own people. We are interested in Israel because of its commitment to human rights. In 1920 a free trade union movement was started there and while the country was still a protectorate under the

League of Nations and under the British mandate, those workers educated their people to freedom, to trade unionism, to an egalitarian spirit—in short, to the exercise of human rights. They believed they would have their own nation and their own freedom. As early as the 1920s, the Israeli Federation of Labour sent representatives here to the United States to sit with the leaders of the AFL to exchange ideas and hopes for the future.

In those early years, the Histadrut, as the General Federation of Labour is known, developed its own systems of social welfare: health and welfare coverage for its people, pensions and retirement homes for retired workers. Over the years, the AFL, and then the AFL-CIO, continued to maintain friendly and fraternal relationships with this burgeoning trade union movement in the State of Israel. We have observed the Israeli labor movement provide the leaders of the state. The first head of the trade union movement in Israel, Ben Gurion, became the first Prime Minister in the State of Israel. Golda Meir, who also became a Prime Minister, was one of Israel's top labor leaders.

We are interested in the State of Israel as we are interested in France, Italy, Great Britain, Norway, Sweden, Denmark, Holland and Luxembourg, as we are interested in some of the emerging nations in Africa. Israel is one of a handful of democracies, one tiny oasis of freedom in a desert of dictatorships and feudal sheikdoms. Today its strong labor movement is led by that staunch, proud unionist Yerucham Meshel. Workers in the Arab lands are not permitted to have free trade unions or free self-expression; they are exploited and oppressed. Little Israel is the only democratic country in that entire region that gives a thriving labor movement an opportunity to exist and prosper.

We must cooperate with all democracies because we assuredly need each other. The only way we can face the threat of Arab oil embargoes and rocketing prices is through collective action. Since they have quadrupled the cost of oil [by early 1980, oil prices had risen by a factor of 16 to 20], the Arab nations have accumulated billions of dollars. They are on their way to bankrupting industrial nations of the western world and only by joining together can we meet their power.

C.

The Belgrade Incident

Excerpts from a speech by Vladimir Bukovsky, the Soviet dissident, to the national convention of the AFL-CIO, Los Angeles, Ca., 1977. The AFL-CIO had also invited five dissidents still living in the U.S.S.R., including Andrei Sakharov. This group was prevented from attending by the Soviet government, in direct contradiction to the Helsinki Accords' provision, signed by the Soviets, guaranteeing "free flow of information and people" across national boundaries.

THE SOLIDARITY OF U.S. LABOR SWUNG OPEN THE DOORS OF MY PRISON CELL

by Vladimir Bukovsky

The Soviet Union has signed various international conventions recognizing the right of workers to strike, but it has not bothered to formulate this right in its own legislation. Moreover, a strike is regarded as a "gross group violation of public order," for which one can be imprisoned for up to three years. This is for a completely peaceful strike, merely for refusal to work. But methods of struggle such as sitdowns, picketing, et cetera, are punished according to the article entitled "mass disorders," with sentences up to fifteen years or the death penalty.

The fictitious Soviet labor unions exist to prevent a real workers' movement from springing up. They do not protect the workers from hunger, arbitrary rules, and exploitation. The labor unions in the USSR are part of the party and governmental apparatus, and they are not concerned with the protection of working people but with the carrying out of party governmental plans.

More than anything else, the Soviet press writes about strikes and unemployment in the West, creating a strange impression among Soviet workers. Many of them seriously believe that you are dying of hunger, because in the Soviet Union only a person facing death from starvation could decide on such a desperate measure as a strike....

Accustomed to lack of rights, Soviet workers prefer to steal from their place of work anything that can be sold on the black market in order somehow to feed their families, but they do not dare make open demands. This is very useful to the authorities, because, in this way everybody is guilty and everybody can be tried, not for his political convictions, but for theft. In general, crime in the country is very widespread, and alcoholism, drug addiction and prostitution flourish.

In all, there are three million prisoners in the country, a little more than one percent of the population. Such a high percentage of convicts is artificially supported by the government, mainly out of economic considerations.

A prisoner is cheap labor, which can easily be shifted by the authorities from one branch of the economy to another, sent to do the most difficult and unprofitable work in underdeveloped parts of the country with a difficult climate, to which free labor could be attracted only by offering very high pay.

But what makes possible the long existence of this huge concentration camp called the Union of Soviet Socialist Republics? Is it only terror and the denial of rights?

I doubt that the creators of the theory of convergence supposed how literally their theory would realize itself!

Soviet prisoners, forced into slave labor, cut down trees and make lumber. The Shah of Iran buys this lumber and uses it in mines where Iranian prisoners work. The British government gets a loan from the Shah of Iran and lends the greater part of it to the Soviet government. For us, however, such paradoxes are no longer news. Beginning with almost the first years of the Soviet regime, over fifty years ago, western businessmen have been helping the communist leadership strengthen its power....

You know better than I that the greatest building projects of the first Five Year Plan were created exclusively with the help of western technology. Every time that the Soviet Union's inefficient economy experiences need—in re-equipment, in support—western countries readily come to its aid. On the one hand, millions of slaves are behind barbed wire eating crusts of bread and in fear of death. On the other hand, well-fed businessmen are completely voluntarily building, strengthening, and enriching this monstrous system of oppression, impossible to compare with anything in history. Why? For what?

My companions in prison

refused to work for the communist system. We, a handful of defenseless people without rights, understood that we could not look people in the eye if we did not refuse to participate in the building of this system. We were deprived of food, we rotted in solitary, we were killed, but we did not back away from our decision. We knew that each ruble they squeezed out of us would turn into bullets—against you in the West—would turn into jails and concentration camps in Russia, Hungary, Czechoslovakia, and it may be, in France, in Germany, in Switzerland. Forgive me my directness and frankness, but I think that I have earned the right to it. I speak for millions of prisoners dying from hunger or scurvy or just killed, and I want to know: what for?...

Some people here in the West try to prove that for people in backward countries the problem of human rights is not as essential as the struggle with poverty. I do not think that these two problems can be separated, because lack of rights gives rise to poverty, and poverty strengthens the lack of rights.

Precisely for this reason the movement for human rights in the Soviet Union, along with purely intellectual rights, defends the rights of workers. More and more workers are joining our movement. They understand that only thus can the vicious circle of lack of rights and poverty be broken....

It is completely evident that western capital investments in the USSR, which are calculated to exploit cheap labor, are directly harmful to the interests of western workers. I am certain that western labor unions at least have the right to investigate all cases of investment of western capital in the USSR, and the conditions of labor and pay in areas where this capital is applied, and I hope that they will not allow profits to be made from the lack of rights of Soviet workers. After all, it is no accident that the final Act of Agreement on Security and Cooperation in Europe, signed in Helsinki, links economic relations with the observance of human rights.

The Helsinki Agreement has created in the USSR and the other countries of eastern Europe a broad movement for its strict observance. In Moscow, in the Ukraine, in Lithuania, in the Caucasus, groups to monitor the observances of the Agreement have been created. Because we knew that the communist countries from the very beginning had no intention to observe the articles dealing with human rights, the members of the Soviet-Helsinki groups collected a considerable body of information on the violations

Left to right, George Meany, Vladimir Bukovsky, Lane Kirkland at 1977 AFL-CIO convention. Chaikin can be seen behind Bukovsky.

of human rights in the USSR and presented this material to the governments of the thirty-five countries signing the Agreement. At present more than half of the members of these groups have been arrested for their activities—such outstanding defenders of human rights as Yuri Orlov, Alexander Ginzburg, Anatole Scharansky, Mykola Rudenko, Zviad Gamsakhurdia, Oleska Tykhyi, and Merab Kostrava....

It looks as if the western countries signed the Helsinki Agreements just for fun, to cover their deals with the Soviet Union with those vague formulas!

Only one voice spoke out in defense of human rights—Chick Chaikin, president of the International Ladies' Garment Workers' Union and your representative at the Belgrade Conference....

Conference on Security and Cooperation in Europe (CSCE), Belgrade, Yugoslavia, November 15, 1977.

The "speaking out" to which Bukovsky refers had occurred a month earlier in mid-November, 1977, at the CSCE, better known as the Belgrade Conference. This was the 35-nation review assembly called for at Helsinki two years earlier, which, among many other provisions, guaranteed to the citizens of the participating countries freedom to travel and to return home.

Chaikin was a "public member" of the U.S. delegation which was headed by Ambassador Arthur J. Goldberg, former Justice of the Supreme Court, Secretary of Labor and U.N. Ambassador, who continuously placed before the conference the failure of the Soviet Union and its satellites, particularly East Germany and Czechoslovakia, to live up to the human rights guarantees in the Helsinki Agreement.

The following U.P.I. report describes the incident. Chaikin's formal statements follow.

BELGRADE, Nov. 15 (UPI)— The Soviet Union accused the United States of "poisoning the atmosphere" at the Belgrade Conference Tuesday after an American union leader asked whether Soviet dissident Andrei Sakharov will be allowed to appear at an AFL-CIO convention next month.

Sol Chaikin, president of the U.S. Ladies' Garment Workers' Union, told the conference that AFL-CIO President Meany mailed invitations to the convention to Sakharov and five other dissidents 10 weeks ago, but the letters never arrived. "It remains to be seen whether individuals and groups who are in the mainstream of American democratic thought can effectively invite Russians with whom they wish to meet."

Soviet delegate Vadim Loginov protested that as "a very sharp attack."

"The representative of the United States insists on poisoning the atmosphere," Loginov said. "It is only the U.S. delegation that is whipping up mistrust and suspicion, whipping up memories of the Cold War."

He cited widespread interference with the mail by U.S. authorities. "The United States should put its own house in order before it comments on the internal affairs of other countries," delegates quoted him as saying.

"Will you or will you not deliver the letters?" Chaikin replied. "Will you or will you not issue a visa so that academician Sakharov might attend the AFL-CIO convention? And will you or will you not permit him to return home to the Soviet Union?"

Chaikin said the United States has stopped denying entry visas to communist union officials to comply with the Helsinki Accords. "Some of the obligations incurred by the Soviet Union in subscribing to the (Helsinki) Final Act do not appear to have been similarly honored," he said.

(Reprinted by permission of United Press International.)

STATEMENT BY MR. SOL CHAIKIN, PUBLIC MEMBER, UNITED STATES DELEGATION TO THE CSCE CONFERENCE, BELGRADE, YUGOSLAVIA, November 15, 1977.

Mr. Chairman,

As we approach the conclusion of our review of implementation of the Declaration of Principles of the Final Act, my delegation wishes to comment further on Principles 9 and 10—concerning Cooperation among States and Fulfillment in good faith of international obligations under international law.

Ambassador Goldberg has already expressed United States views on some important aspects of the implementation of Principle 10, in particular, in his statement on language of the Final Act which asserts: "In exercising their sovereign rights, including the right to determine their laws and regulations...(the participating states) will conform with their legal obligations under international law."

Earlier in our review, Professor Hughes also spoke of the implementation of these same principles and noted some difficulties that had arisen in the period since the signing of the Final Act.

Like Professor Hughes I am a private citizen and not a professional diplomat. I am president of a large, well-known national union, and in addition I have the honor and responsibility to be a vice-president of the AFL-CIO. I represent many millions of free trade union members of the United States, who, together with their families, make up a tremendous body of public opinion in our country. Today I wish to discuss matters falling within the purview of the Final Act that are of direct interest to all of them and, thus, to our Government.

But first let us recall some of the precise language of Principles 9 and 10. It was agreed at Helsinki, in the context of cooperation among states, that the CSCE participants "confirm that governments, institutions, organizations and *persons* have a relevant and positive role to play in contributing toward the achievement of these aims of their cooperation." In pledging to honor their obligations under international law, the participating states specifically defined their obligations as those "arising from the generally recognized principles and rules of international law and those obligations arising from treaties *or other agreements*, in conformity with international law, to which they are a party." Moreover, in their promises at Helsinki to fulfill in good faith their obligations under international law, all participants reaffirmed the primacy of their obligations to the Charter of the United Nations.

Mr. Chairman, the American people are looking upon our discussions at Belgrade with the expectation that we can have a frank and full exchange of views on the implementation of the Final Act to date and with the hope that we can agree on further concrete measures to strengthen the CSCE process and its contribution to the overall construction of detente.

In the period since August 1975, my own country, which openly acknowledges its imperfections and seeks to correct them, has endeavored to bring its policies and practices fully into conformity with the Final Act. In this effort, the Congress of the United States has this year enacted legislation to facilitate the issuance of visas to members of communist trade unions. This legislation, I think I do not need to emphasize, has not been universally popular among all of us in the United States. But it is now the law of the land, a solemn obligation of my Government, and it is honored.

I regret to say, however, that on the other hand some of the obligations incurred by the Soviet Union in subscribing to above mentioned precepts of the Final Act do not appear to have been similarly honored.

Mr. Chairman, I have with me a copy of an invitation addressed on September 6 by President George Meany of the AFL-CIO to Academician Andre Sakharov, winner of the Nobel Prize and fearless champion of human rights, and five other Soviet citizens to attend a convention of the AFL-CIO in December. This invitation was sent from Washington to Academician Sakharov and the other invitees in early September through the ordinary mail. But what has transpired since then is a mystery. We cannot confirm that the invitation ever reached Mr. Sakharov, nor has Mr. Meany ever received a reply.

After sending these invitations, Mr. Meany wrote to President Carter asking his help in encouraging the Soviet authorities to issue exit visas for our invited guests and of course to allow them to return home. Since we have changed our own visa policies, it remains to be seen whether individuals and groups who are in the mainstream of U.S. democratic thought can effectively invite Russians with whom they wish to meet.

I might add that the U.S. Embassy in Moscow has sent a formal diplomatic note to the Soviet Ministry of Foreign Affairs officially supporting Mr. Meany's invitation to Mr. Sakharov. Yet uncertainty continues to cloud the question of whether Mr. Sakharov is permitted to receive his mail from Mr. Meany and to dispatch a reply, and whether the visas will be issued.

This appears to be a clear-cut violation of the "Freedom of Transit" guarantees of the Universal

Postal Convention and thus a failure to honor obligations under international law and the Final Act. If this is so, and it certainly appears to be, then the obvious result will be for many millions of Americans to conclude that our unilateral change in visa policy has failed to persuade the Soviet authorities to ameliorate theirs. This could only, in many minds in our own country, cast doubt upon our own great efforts to perfect compliance with the Final Act.

Mr. Chairman, I cite this case not to damage the atmosphere of this important meeting at Belgrade but to attempt to ascertain what has happened to a piece of mail sent from my country to a distinguished citizen of the Soviet Union. If there is an explanation of what has transpired, my delegation would be most eager to hear it. In the meantime, we feel obliged to draw attention to what appears to be a violation of pledges undertaken by all of us in Principles 9 and 10 of the Final Act.

May I conclude by reiterating what has often been stressed here at Belgrade by Ambassador Goldberg— namely that the American people, and certainly this is true of U.S. workers, will only support the process of detente provided the process is humane and just, and if solemn pledges, like those endorsed at Helsinki at the highest level, are truly respected.

In their reply, the delegates from the Soviet Union, together with those from Czechoslovakia and the GDR (East Germany), did not speak to the charges; the AFL-CIO letter to Sakharov was not referred to. They accused Chaikin of "poisoning the atmosphere." He was permitted the right of reply.

RIGHT OF REPLY STATEMENT BY MR. CHAIKIN
November 15, 1977

Mr. Chairman, my country does not yield to any other in its intense and abiding desire to implement and strengthen the principles of the Final Act.

We reject the contention, however, that a

169

dialogue relating to implementation poisons the atmosphere. On the contrary, it will strengthen our objectives, notwithstanding the fact that some countries are unaccustomed to it, or embarrassed by it. *We are here to review the implementation of the Principles agreed to*—to see how they are working out. We do not agree that a proper "understanding" of this review means that we must avoid mention of any violations of the Principles.

Mr. Chairman, I have listened to the response from the distinguished representatives of the Soviet Union and the German Democratic Republic and I have waited in vain to hear a clear, simple, response to my question, relating to the Sakharov letter. Instead of dialogue, we have diversion and other non-responsive accusations. Could we not now have an answer? Five separate letters were mailed September 6. It is now November 15th. Will you or will you not deliver the letters? Will you or will you not issue a visa so that Academician Sakharov might attend the AFL-CIO convention? Will you or will you not permit him to return home to the Soviet Union?

D.
The U.S.A. And Britain Share A Commitment

General Conference of the National Union of Tailors and Garment Workers, Scarborough, England, April 23, 1979.

The greatest single value England and the United States

hold in common, regardless of occasional differences in other matters, is our complete devotion to human rights. We oppose tyranny everywhere. When we discussed Chile and the deprivation of political, human and trade union rights there, we talked as well about Czechoslovakia, where there is also deprivation of human rights. When we talked about the military dictatorship in Argentina that daily grinds workers into the earth, we also looked toward East Germany and noted its lack of political democracy and free trade unions.

Human rights has been a topical issue in the last year or two, made a little more popular by our President, Jimmy Carter. But we trade unionists from the U.S.A. have been standard bearers for a universal system of human rights for more than a hundred years, and you in Great Britain have been espousing the cause even longer.

We share your devotion. We share your commitment. It is a commitment to democracy and to the millions who defend democracy.

E.

A Chilean Chronicle

**Press interview,
Santiago, Chile, May 23, 1978.**

In May 1978, AFL-CIO vice-presidents Thomas W. Gleason, president of the International Longshoremen's Association (ILA), and Sol Chick Chaikin, president of the International Ladies' Garment Workers' Union (ILGWU), together with other AFL-CIO representatives, undertook a "solidarity visit" to Chile. It was four and one-half years since the military coup that had overthrown the previous Allende government. Their purpose was to interpose the prestige and influence of the AFL-CIO between the remnants of the free trade unions in Chile and the leaders of the current repressive regime. They planned to express to President Augusto Pinochet the AFL-CIO's deep interest in the restoration of full human rights in Chile.

Members of the "Group of Ten" or "Dinamicos," had come to the AFL-CIO pleading for help against arbitrary arrests, beatings and the exiling of trade unionists. They represented approximately 350,000 workers in ten separate unions. Fearful that General Pinochet was preparing once again to move against this remaining core of free, democratic trade unionists, George Meany acted to pressure the military junta into resorting trade union rights. Before the trip, two Chilean ships loaded with perishables were boycotted by the ILA, a token gesture to suggest the more severe sanctions the union was capable of enforcing. At the conclusion of their two-day mission, Gleason and Chaikin were interviewed by the Chilean press.

MR. GLEASON: Since Monday morning, we have met with various groups, all representing Chilean labor. Yesterday afternoon we met with President Pinochet and his ministers and for two hours we discussed in great detail the problems concerning free trade unionism here in Chile.

My friend and fraternal delegate, Mr. Sol Chick Chaikin, will take over and explain the points we discussed. Brother Chaikin...

MR. CHAIKIN: For 25 years or more, officers of the AFL-CIO have been intimately involved with the evolution of the trade union movement in your great country, Chile. We are thoroughly aware of political and trade union developments and we understand the present Chilean reality.

We have come to Chile at the invitation of the Group of Ten and we are their guests. With their understanding we have attempted to expand the area of our visit and contacts. As a result, we have met with other democratically-oriented trade unionists. We are aware of differences among these various groups, but discovered what indeed they must know: Their areas of agreement in the practice of free trade unionism outweigh whatever differences they have described to us. We are encouraged that the sentiment for the exercise of free trade union rights is much more widespread than we had thought.

We want to make it plain to the citizens of this country, as we have to General Pinochet, that we do not consider our presence here in any way an intervention into your internal affairs. For more than one hundred years in our own country, citizens of the United States have fought to develop a system of free trade unionism, and we believe that such a movement is the very foundation of any system of human rights. It is our further conviction that the quest for full human rights is universal. Borders, walls, or other obstructions cannot be built or created—physically or spiritually—that can keep the idea of human rights from pervading every country, every culture, every society around this world. Since we are concerned with the basis for the establishment of a human rights system, namely a free trade union movement, we consider our visit an extension of that concern.

We reminded President Pinochet that we represented the greatest national free trade union center in the world. We conversed for two hours in a friendly, non-adversary exchange. We defined what we and our Chilean friends meant by the words "free trade union rights": The right of assembly without prior permission; the right of workers freely to choose their own representatives; the right of these leaders to bargain collectively with their employers for and on behalf of the workers they represent; and in those unusual circumstances where workers and employers are unable to agree, if all else fails, the right of the workers to strike.

Above all, there must be no control of the trade union movement by any political party, no intervention of management in the affairs of the union, no control by the Church and, indeed, no intervention on the part of the government. We said the word "free" was readily understood, it was a word that had universal meaning and was not subject to tampering.

There was full discussion. President Pinochet declared himself in complete agreement with our definition of a free trade union movement but then imparted some definitions of his own with which we were not in agreement.

To our urging that he begin the process of respect for democratic institutions and lift restriction on the operations of free trade unions, his response was it would be done, but he needed time. We suggested that time was not the friend of this administration, that the AFL-CIO was not unhappy at the fall of the Allende government, since we were aware of the conditions of this unhappy country at the time of the military coup. While, if we were citizens of Chile, we might have preferred some other eventuality, still we were content to give the new government an opportunity to ameliorate distress, correct excesses and return the country to democratic rule. We have written this government, our trade union brothers have petitioned this government, and we have been patient indeed. The President said this was just a transitory stage; we remarked that one man's transitory stage was another man's lifetime and that each of us on this earth had only one such lifetime.

We attempted to point out that we were aware that some restrictions were being lifted in other areas of national life. We believed, therefore, it was time to lift some restrictions from a sector of national life which was most important not only to the workers involved but also to the country generally.

The President stated that some time in the future he planned to encourage collective bargaining; it would be the first change. We responded that, without prior free elections of union representatives, collective bargaining is a sham and would not have the meaning to democratically-inclined people he believed it might.

We urged him again and again to consider free elections of union representatives. We pointed out that in other areas of national life, such as among employer groups and cooperatives, ministers were encouraging elections and that our union brothers and sisters of Chile should have the same right now.

We attempted to make one important point. We tried to explain to the President and his ministers that efforts to suppress a free trade union movement would not be helpful to his objectives and his desires for the people of Chile. The longer this repression continues, the more the majority of workers, who are committed today to the democratic ideal, would be driven through desperation, frustration, and lack of hope to desert this ideal. They would be pushed to one extreme or the other until the democratic alternative would stand a good chance of being destroyed. There would be a replay in this country of what has occurred in other countries where, in the absence of a broad citizenship practicing democracy, only the two extremes of right and left remain to confront each other, to the detriment of every citizen.

We asked why it was not possible for the American Institute for Free Labor Development, AIFLD, the co-workers of our brothers and sisters in the free, democratic trade union movement of Chile, to conduct seminars and institutes to train union representatives or would-be union representatives in the ideals and techniques of a democratic, free union movement. The President said the government was engaged in the training of such officers. Again we pointed out that this was indeed useless since a trade union movement controlled and governed by leaders of the government was not worthy of its name and was unacceptable. If he favors the eventual establishment of a free, democratic trade union movement, the president need not worry when young leaders are trained by AIFLD. We stated what is well-known universally and uncontested: that the single, most powerful force against the extremes of authoritarian government—whether Marxist, Fascist or "directed-democracy" [as the Chilean government describes itself]— is the AFL-CIO, the organization we represent. The President responded that he had no objection if we were to conduct these seminars and institutes and turned to his ministers and repeated that statement.

We assured President Pinochet that, as representatives of the AFL-CIO, upon our return we would make a full report to the leaders of our union movement and to the highest levels of our American government as well and we would regret to have to inform them of what we perceived to be the lack of progress in restoring trade union rights, so basic to any acceptable system of human rights.

We spent some time with the ministers who remained after the President departed. We suggested that a very useful purpose would be served if they would agree, from time to time, to receive a delegation of trade union leaders from the Group of Ten and from one or two of the other groups with whom we had met. Many misunderstandings could be cleared up if communication were open and direct. Our hope was that they would make themselves available for a dialogue with representatives of the free trade union movement in Chile.

REPORTER: I would like to ask if you discussed with the President of the Republic anything about trade union liberties as a base for collective bargaining?

MR. CHAIKIN: Much of the two-hour discussion related to trade union liberties. The President repeated time and again his feeling that trade union liberty should be established and encouraged. We had two difficulties with his statements. The first was that *we* were talking about *now*, or if not now, then in three or four months. The President was talking about some indefinite time in the future.

The second difficulty was that although we were using the same words, they did not have the same meaning. To us, free trade unionism means that the workers freely choose their representatives. To the President it seemed to mean that a free trade union movement was one wherein the leaders are chosen or trained by the government and, at some future time, after being installed, would be free to go about their appointed responsibilities.

I responded that we were playing with words. Labor leaders who are chosen by the government and appointed by the government are no more free than a child given birth by a mother and raised by a mother, is free from a mother's influence.

Even under the best of circumstances, we did not expect the President to agree yesterday that our requests should go into effect today. We believe this government should have a reasonable time to reflect upon the meaning of our solidarity visit, to ponder the reasonable suggestions we believe we made, to consider whether this process of loosening the ties in various sectors of national life should not further proceed with lifting some restrictions from the trade union movement.

We believe this government should have time to consider very seriously the adverse effects on public opinion in the United States of a continued disregard for traditional democratic rights and continued repression of a free trade union movement. Our preconceived notions and opinions were minimal. Our present opinions are a result of dialogue and observation. So far as our major interest on behalf of free trade unionism is concerned, our final opinion will depend in most part on the response of your government to the suggestions we have made.

>REPORTER: You who are so addicted to free trade unionism, and criticize some aspects of what happened here in Chile, what is your idea about what is happening to free trade unionism on the world scene?

MR. CHAIKIN: We are distressed at every incident that lessens the opportunity for the practice of free trade unionism. We are distressed at the nature of totalitarian governments which, almost from the first day of their accession to power, seek to destroy the free trade union movement. We view with distress the number of countries where the elite, the owners of the land, mines, mills and factories, the controllers of the financial life of communities, seek to protect their own position, using their political influence to destroy opportunities for free trade unions.

We in the AFL-CIO have been in the forefront of the fight against aggressive, oppressive communism which, through force of arms, has darkened the lights of freedom and of free trade unionism in the eastern nations of Europe and in a number of other countries and which recently was on the way to extinguishing the lights of freedom in your own country and which is now engaged in adventurism on the continent of Africa.

>REPORTER: From the Latin American and Chilean experience in the trade union movement, are you in agreement that the trade union movement should not only make economic demands but be active in a political sense?

MR. CHAIKIN: Let me tell you only the philosophy of the U.S. trade union movement, which is shared in varying degrees with trade union movements of other western industrial nations.

We believe that the first and foremost allegiance of trade union leaders is to the workers they represent. The primary concern of these leaders should be the well-being of the workers within the frame of reference of their employment. But union workers are also citizens of the communities in which they live, as union leaders are also citizens of these communities, and they may not be denied the average and ordinary privileges and responsibilities of citizenship. We believe that the union itself must not be ideologically oriented, nor controlled by the ideology of a political party, but individual members of the union are free in the exercise of their personal citizenship, to identify with any political party and are free to differ politically among themselves as to the general practices and theory of government.

We firmly believe that a trade union movement should be primarily concerned with matters of wages, hours and working conditions. It should be concerned with the best interests of the workers they represent on the job, but they cannot be so antiseptic, they cannot be so sterile, they cannot be so removed from all of the other processes of society as to make them second-class citizens.

> REPORTER: In your conversation with President Pinochet, did you touch on the problem of the trade union leaders who were exiled and afterwards were removed from their union positions and thrown out of their jobs?

MR. CHAIKIN: Yes, we did. We expressed our belief that government interposition in the affairs of the unions is unacceptable except where a union or its leaders are proven, as a result of due process, to be acting against the law.

The abrupt removal of trade union leaders, formally elected, is just as reprehensible to free trade unionism as is the appointment of union leaders. We further pointed out to the General that many of these individuals are suffering because of government action. Union leaders in Chile have been removed from their union positions, and, in an act of cruel and unusual punishment, have been removed from their jobs as well. Even worse is the practice of banishment, something relatively unknown in the last decades except in other repressive totalitarian governments, like the Soviet Union and Cuba.

(Reprinted with permission from the AFL-CIO Free Trade Union News, *Vol. 33, #11, Nov. 1978, p.6-8.)*

President Jimmy Carter and Sol Chick Chaikin
(Photo by Steve Yarmola, AFL-CIO)

ILGWU Executive Board meeting
Hollywood, Fla., January 4, 1980.

As you will recall, the two significant events of our trip to Chile were these: We had the first public meeting without prior government permission, and second, we arranged a public press conference supportive of democratic trade union leaders.

As the solidarity team prepared to leave, a member of the "Group of Ten" said to us, "You came for only two days but you created a hurricane. We feel the time is right to do something, to make a beginning." But it has been a slow beginning.

Following our visit, AIFLD seminars were reinstituted and some Chilean union leaders were permitted to attend. In November 1979, representatives of the Group of Ten attended the AFL-CIO convention in Washington, D.C. In January 1980 a large copper mine was struck, suggesting that Chilean workers are more secure and willing to take risks for democratic principles.

Despite these positive signs, the Pinochet regime continues to be relentless in its opposition to free trade unionism as we know it here. It oppresses and persecutes democratic trade unionists. We remain hopeful that the indomitable spirit of those courageous enough to stand up against the government will help gain the inevitable victory. In that struggle they can count on our support.

F.
Statement On The Indo-Chinese Refugees

Labor Summit,
Tokyo, Japan, June 22, 1979.
To Prime Minister Masayoshi Ohira of Japan.

Mr. Prime Minister, permit me now to make a presentation solely as the representative of the AFL-CIO, the great national labor center of the United States.

My wife and I were privileged to be guests at the White House state dinner given in your honor last month by our President, Jimmy Carter. As you spoke, we recognized in you a man of reason and compassion, and with great concern for the sanctity of the human personality.

I plead with you, and with the government you represent, to act boldly and generously in regard to the plight of the Indo-Chinese refugees! Open your heart and your country to them! Save from disaster as many as possible.

Japan is a great country, and great is the refugee's need. The world will applaud your positive response to this enormous problem. We here assembled are representatives of free men and women.

Your affirmative and timely action in concert with other nations will advance our mutual and just cause.

Thank you, Mr. Prime Minister.

G.

A Clarion Call From The White House

**Friends of Carter-Mondale Dinner,
Washington, D.C., October 24, 1979.**

...When the record of this Administration is writ, all of the things that come to mind quickly will not loom so large as the fact that from this bully pulpit, from the Office of the President of the United States, has gone out the clear call for the observance of human rights for every living being upon this great world of ours. Inevitably, no matter what the near future may bring, decades from now, when our children and grandchildren leaf through the history books, it will be noted in the accounts of the nations that during these past few years and hopefully for many years to come, a cry went out for the celebration of the human personality, for decency, for humanity, no matter the color, no matter the creed, no matter the station of life and that clarion call came from Jimmy Carter's White House.

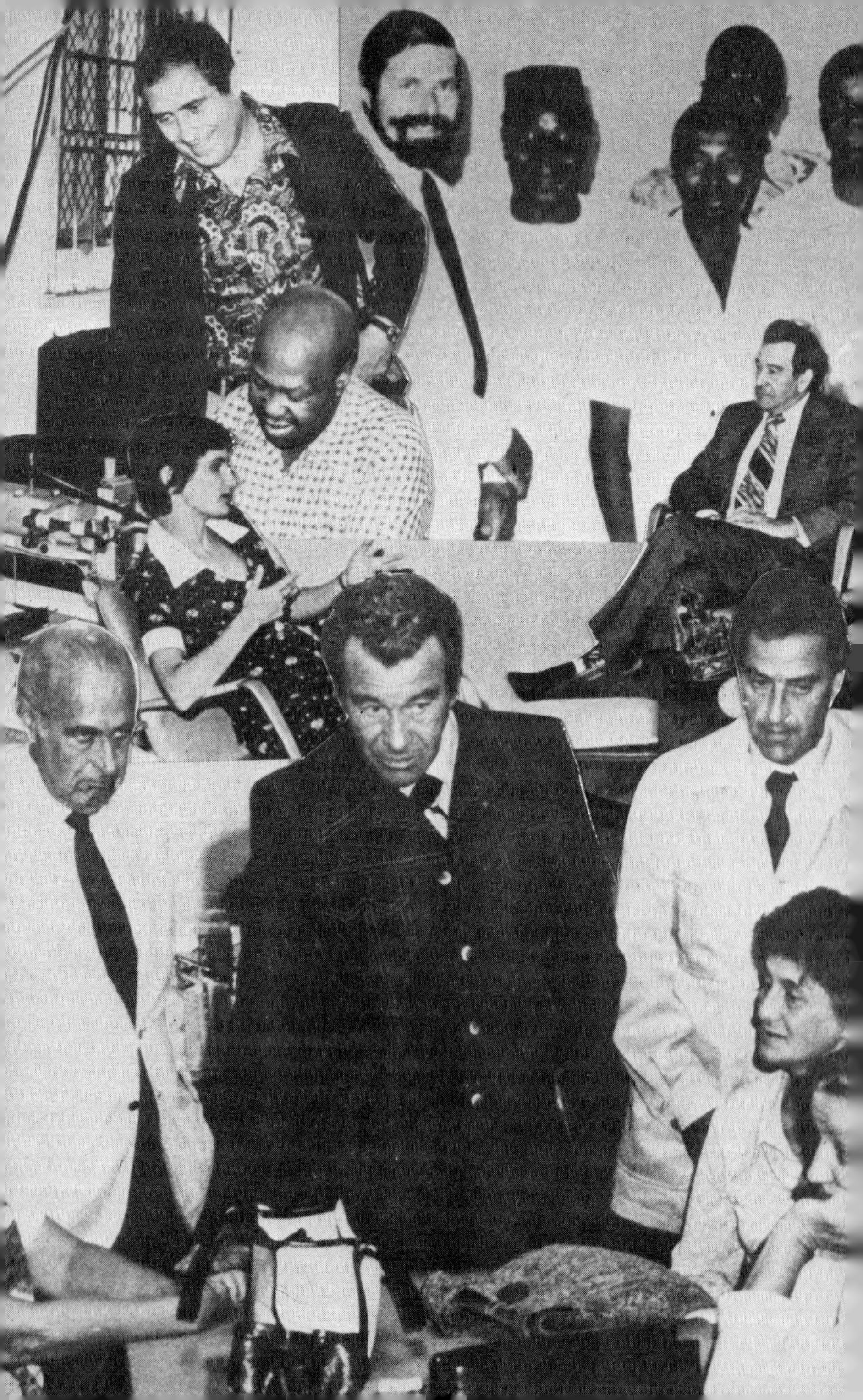

ICAN TRADE UNION

TIONAL
T WORKERS UN

part three

PULLING TOGETHER:
AN AGENDA FOR AMERICA

I am saddened when I remember how often labor's support for now-accepted social goals turned into unnecessarily long, lonely and bitter fights because U.S. power centers did not learn where our common interests lay.

Diverse interests pulling in different and often selfish directions are tearing this country apart. Despite conflicting aims, we must all harness our energies and pull together to make our society work. A consensus of the broad majority must be recreated.

Our system of democratic populist capitalism, continuously monitored, with excesses speedily corrected, is the best hope we in labor see for bringing the greatest good to the greatest number. It needs criticism and improvement and we see a vast unfinished agenda for America.

Sol Chick Chaikin

one

We Face Complex Challenges

A.

**Cornell University,
November 13, 1978, Weinberg Seminar.**

**Executive Program at Arden House, Harriman, N.Y.,
Columbia University, June 14, 1979,
[statistics up-dated to January 1980].**

We in the U.S. labor movement are committed to the operation of a free, democratic capitalist society. But we know, perhaps better than our employers, that this system would have fallen years ago were it not for the work of the U.S. trade union movement, were it not for our shoring-up efforts in our fight for the supports to keep the economy going.

I believe that free, democratic, competitive capitalism is the best system yet devised to give full opportunity for creative intelligence, hard work and risk taking, to provide us all with more material benefits as well as greater liberty and justice. But the excesses of capitalism must be tempered by the vigilance of a vital free trade union movement and must be subject to government interposition and oversight on behalf of those with the least.

The capitalist system does not, on its own, provide steady

opportunities for work nor fair distribution of the wealth produced; it needs constant correction so that no one will be left out.

This system has not been able to deliver full employment: Not everyone who wants to work can find a job—nor does every job provide a living wage. Despite our efforts to alleviate economic hardship in our country, 11 percent of all Americans still live in poverty, as defined, not by the U.S. trade union movement, but by the government. Moreover, were it not for all the social programs unions have fought for through the years—aid to the blind, to dependent children, to widows and orphans, Social Security, survivorship benefits, unemployment compensation, food stamps, welfare payments, and more—if not for these, one in four families would suffer severe economic hardship. Without these union-supported public programs, nearly one in two of our black brothers and sisters would be impoverished.

How long could the capitalist system have lasted without the social welfare improvements for which the U.S. trade union movement persevered? Bear in mind that other political systems in the world are all too willing to seduce our disaffected and dispossessed. Men and women with no stake in our country have nothing to lose in following any Pied Piper who promises a better life. You cannot eat democracy, you cannot wear democracy, nor will it keep you warm on a cold winter's night. If we fail to make democratic capitalism work so that all our citizens are well-fed, well-clothed and well-housed, then democracy is merely a thin label that camouflages naked self-interest and is not deserving of our loyalty.

The U.S. labor movement sees a vast unfinished agenda for the United States and invites everyone—for it will take everyone—to join us in building a more democratic, more prosperous nation. The challenges we confront are complex and the agenda is long, but let me begin with the two most vexing problems facing not only the United States but all the western industrialized nations and Japan: the persistent afflictions of unemployment and inflation. How we handle these twin nemeses will mark all our lives for many years to come.

We all agree that unemployment is bad, inflation is bad, poverty is bad, but about what to do there is no agreement. Even the country's leading economists differ on the causes and cures and, indeed, our Nobel Laureates offer opposite remedies. Perhaps, then, a trade unionist should speak only in vague generalities or avoid the issues altogether. I do think, though, that our economy is possibly too complicated to be left in the hands of our economists. My plan here is, in the words of Spinoza, to discuss "not the meaning of the words, but the nature of things."

Inflation is world-wide. Although situations differ and patterns differ, no country has coped effectively. It has made no difference apparently that Germany has been governed by Social Democrats with Helmut Schmidt, an accomplished economist, as Chancellor, while Giscard d'Estaing, also a distinguished economist, has represented the Center Right in French politics. The inflation rate in Germany is running 5.9 percent and in France 12.4 percent. It has made no difference that Jim Callaghan, the former British Prime Minister, represented socialists derived from the old Fabians, supported by the British Labour Party, while Margaret Thatcher, the new Prime Minister, is a Conservative. Indeed, although her proposals differ substantially from Callaghan's, I would hazard the guess that high inflation will continue under her government. [The Consumer Price Index in the United Kingdom rose from 7.8 percent on October 1978 to 17.2 percent one year later.]

Here in the United States we have had Republican administrations followed by Jimmy Carter's administration and we have seen little difference whether the Council of Economic advisors was chaired by Gardner Ackley and Arthur M. Okun under President Johnson; Paul McCracken, Herbert Stein or Allen Greenspan under Nixon and Ford; or Charles Schultze in the staff under Eisenhower and Johnson and now resurrected by Jimmy Carter. The problem is the same and no one has come up with a solution: High and sustained unemployment in all the western industrialized nations exists side by side with high and sustained inflation.

Prices rising during a downturn have happened before, but not as much. This new disorder under the industrial sun has a new name: stagflation, a combination of *stagnation* because our growth has slowed and *inflation* because prices have risen sharply. Traditional economists have always offered unemployment as the cure for inflation, but since 1970, against all predictions, we have suffered from both. Our inflation rate ran 9 percent from December 1978 to December 1979. At the start of 1980 the rate on an annual basis is about 18 percent. Our unemployment is about 6.2 percent, up from 5.8 percent. Let us examine unemployment and inflation separately.

B.
Unemployment/ Full Employment

Columbia University, June 14, 1979.

By December, 1978, this administration had reduced unemployment from 8 percent at the end of 1976 to 5.9 percent. We in the AFL-CIO have had some experience with government figures and know that unemployment is much higher in this country than the official figures suggest. We are aware, for example, that normally 1.0 to 1.5 percent of the employables—some 1 million people who are ready, willing and able to work—are not counted in the unemployed figures because they believe that work is not available in their communities. They often live in small towns and have gone from shop to shop and door to door in search of work. They need waste no more time in this way because the scuttlebutt tells them that whatever new factories remain in their communities are not now hiring. They have given up, frustrated and aggravated. Some bureaucrat in Washington has decided that such desperate human beings are no longer counted in the labor force as "unemployed." It is as though that bureaucrat had taken a red marking pencil and drawn a line through their lives—through more than a million lives. But each one is a living, breathing human being who would work and would contribute if there were jobs.

We also know, in spite of a little pickup in business, that too many Americans are working part-time because of work shortages. They are under-employed and represent a portion of unemployment as well. Some groups in our labor force, such as blacks and youths, have a far higher unemployment rate than does the general labor force. What a fearful toll that takes; a generation raised to know only despair and confusion.

Nevertheless, we in labor agree that under the Carter administration the jobless figure was knocked down. Some two million more people were employed. How was this done? In my judgment it was because a program that expressed the best thinking of the AFL-CIO was presented to and accepted in part by the Executive and the Congress. We maintained that a coordinated program was necessary to attack the problem of unemployment. We were not the only ones with the one true faith and sole clear vision. Many people agreed with us and many of them were legislators.

These were some of the key programs we proposed: First, we suggested a public works program, combined with public service employment, a Comprehensive Employment and Training Act, CETA, where people could be hired to work in town, village or city. Second, we wanted to target several billion dollars for special youth training, to aid many of the young adults who graduated from high school in the terrible recession of 1974-75 and have not worked a single month since then. After so much idle time, these young people have very few skills and even less motivation to achieve. Third, we proposed a large and sustained program to create additional dwellings, including the rehabilitation of much housing. Fourth, we argued, surprisingly to some, that certain investment tax credits ought to be continued, even increased. We made a study, which was supplemented by consultation with government, some

Chambers of Commerce and employers' associations, and it showed that too many of our plants and machines were excessively old and require a sustained effort to refurbish or replenish them. Today in the United States we are producing too much with machinery built 30 or more years ago. Hardly 20 percent of our plant and equipment is less than seven or eight years of age, while many factories in Hong Kong, Taiwan and Germany are brand new and super-efficient.

We must put people back to work. It is eminently worthwhile to salvage human beings, to assure that they are contributing members of our society, and surely it is worthwhile from the point of view of our pocketbooks. For every 1 percent of unemployment in the United States, the taxpayers shell out $16 billion in welfare payments, Medicaid, unemployment compensation and all the other necessary social welfare programs. The business community has a further stake in full employment. Unemployment means not only human misery, but also lost consumer-buying power, lost business sales, high overhead costs and low levels of investment in plants and equipment.

Full employment should be our primary national goal; it solves most economic and human problems. As a people, we do not think it can be done. But we might begin by remembering the history of our successes. There is, for example, a misremembering of the New Deal's record in dealing with the unemployment of the 1929-32 collapse. President Roosevelt is generally faulted for failing to restore a healthy economy until World War II. Nothing could be further from the truth. The bottom of the depression came in 1933, with the incredible, shameful unemployment rate of 24 percent—one of every four workers were out of a job! New Deal programs reduced that to about 14 percent in 1937. That is, they cut the rate nearly in half—44 percent—and 5.1 million went back to work.

Then came the recession of 1937. Why? Because New Deal programs were cut back just when they should have been expanded. The Federal budget was reduced instead of enlarged. The results were predictable: a downturn, hurting not only the workers but the very people who had cried out loudest against

New Deal programs.

We are not amateurs, as they were in 1933. We have had more than 40 years of experience in how to put people to work to maintain a healthy economy. They succeeded in 1933 and it is time, it is long past time, to put our experience and knowledge to work.

The AFL-CIO's proposed program would have cost $30 billion in 1977, and we knew $30 billion in one year was a great deal of money, but we considered it the best possible use of money and absolutely necessary.

At first the Carter administration said, "Yes, we know we have to prime the pump. Yes, we know we have to meet these needs. But we have other concerns and we had better get going on our major one: balancing the budget by 1981."

Against spending $30 billion to tackle unemployment, there were countervailing pressures for a tax cut to put some money back into the hands of people who are working and paying taxes. The theory was that people would take their tax rebates and quickly spend the money, creating a demand for goods and services that would get the wheels going. We in labor knew that tax rebates did not work that simply. People do not always rush out to spend those few dollars. Furthermore, job creation is always more efficient than cutting taxes. We have more than 40 years' experience to demonstrate that we do not get the bang out of the tax rebate buck that we get from a dollar spent on direct job creation.

It is estimated that it takes $40,000 of tax rebate money to develop one job whereas a direct expenditure from the government of perhaps $10,000 would go the full way towards creating a single job, a 4 to 1 ratio. That is, we can make about four times as many jobs spending our dollars directly on job creation than indirectly on tax rebates. The quickest way to get work for people is to put them to work.

Job creation would be especially helpful toward the President's goal of balancing the budget. There would be far fewer tax-eaters—that is, people collecting unemployment compensation, collecting welfare, engaging in crimes—and far more taxpayers.

Jimmy Carter accepted many of our proposals and put forward a $30-$31 billion program that could be phased in over two years, rather than one. Then the Gross National Product began growing at a rate faster than expected. Whether this was the result of natural ebullience after the change of administration, whether it was the result of some pent-up purchasing power that was already around, or whether it was one of those unpredictable decisions American consumers sometimes make, everyone seemed to wake up on the same day with a desire to spend a few dollars. It became apparent that the economy was beginning to reflate a little and a tax rebate was not the way to go.

The tax cut of 1977 went by the board and the rest of our program was halved. Still, it is my guess that some progress was made in knocking down unemployment because of the federal government's programs, since two million returned to work. I think the administration should have gone for our full program so that the country would have been ahead of the game, a little stronger, a little more able to deal with whatever the future might bring. We would have brought unemployment down to the 5 percent or 4.5 percent range where it ought to be this year, instead of 6.2 where it is at present.

If we had increased overall productivity in this country, that is the amount of goods and services produced, we would have been better able to deal with the second scourge, inflation.

C.
The Scourge Of Inflation

Columbia University, June 14, 1979.

In the labor movement we have always been aware that,

along with unemployment, inflation is the second of our twin evils. Inflation robs us of every gain, now and for the future: We are its prime victims.

After the First World War and during the great depression, workers had very little. All they had, if they were gainfully employed, were their jobs; they had almost no equity in the country. Literally, they had only their hands, their minds, and their eyes. "Workers of the world, unite!" was one slogan they could react to, not in its political sense, but as it called for a union of purpose. Working for a common employer, wanting to have something to say about their wages and working conditions, they joined hands to build unions. Over the years these unions struggled and negotiated with reasonable success. When you look at the U.S. working class today, you see one of the nation's greatest strengths.

Separate and apart from hourly earnings, union members now have equity. Many are covered by retirement plans; nearly all workers can look forward to Social Security. We have a stake in the value of the dollar; we put present-day dollars into a pension fund with the expectation that the future dollars we collect will have strong purchasing power. It would be a fool's paradise for us to put our hard-won dollars into a pension fund today and twenty years from now take out worthless dimes. We have struggled over decades for some job security and a measure of reasonable comfort when our working days are over; we must not permit our struggles to come to naught.

We are also concerned about the few dollars we may have in savings banks. Working people are not risk-takers; generally our wages are not so high that we can take chances. Savings banks are attractive to us, yet we watch the value of our savings shrink there. We are concerned about the life insurance savings many of us have. It is not a great amount, but it is some small measure of security for the people we leave behind. So we are grievously worried about inflation; working people have a stake in stability.

We in labor always have been concerned with the inflationary aspects of national policy. Yet, philosophically, there comes a point of departure between us and many other people in the community. If it were a question of a trade-off between human misery—unemployment—or embarking on programs where we might expect a little higher inflation rate of ½ to 1 percent a year for a year or two, we would always be found arguing for the slightly inflationary programs that help people as against those that may have a deflationary aspect and destroy people: unemployment.

In the past, unemployment was the solution of choice among traditional economists for coping with inflation. With stagflation, even high unemployment has not budged high inflation. The inhumane solution does not work; perhaps humane ones will be tried.

Five parts of inflation

For the year 1979, our burgeoning inflation is running at the rate of 13 percent, up from 9 percent one year ago. Although wage increases are often blamed—the so-called wage-push theory—the major push for price increases are in energy, food, housing, medical care and interest rates. There are other price increases, but the main push has been occurring in those five sectors.

The Carter administration, when it came to office, stated that it was going to concentrate on the Big Problem in the United States—unemployment. Now they say the Number One Domestic Problem is inflation. We have no serious quarrel with that viewpoint so long as they reiterate that we still are troubled with excessive and sustained unemployment: some six million out of work.

We do not believe this inflation is the result of a wage push. Energy, food, housing, medical care and interest rates are almost completely unaffected by what the AFL-CIO and its component unions have done, even including the hospital workers who daily struggle to get just a little better break for themselves. In fact, the average hospital workers makes $80 less a week than the average factory worker. Most of the labor-intensive products that make up the Consumer Price Index have gone up very little. In our own industry, for example, in textile and apparel, where some of the most highly labor-intensive products are made, the price increases have averaged 2 to 3 percent per year.

The price of oil and gas has skyrocketed, but wages in petroleum refining amount to about 2 cents a gallon. The cost of a house is now beyond the reach of most working people. Yet the labor costs are only 17 percent of the price of 1977's average $57,300 house—and this is way down from 1949 when on-site labor was 31 percent of the cost of the then-average $9,455 house.

No, this is not a wage-push inflation. Between 1972 and 1979, consumer prices rose 74 percent, dividends climbed 114 percent, interest payments soared 157 percent, profits after taxes topped them all at a 161 percent rise, but weekly wages after taxes rose only 64 percent.

Despite this evidence, the administration plan of last October set forth a so-called price and wage guideline program. Wages were indeed guided but prices, for all practical purposes, were permitted to roam free. Wage increases were explicitly limited to 7 percent, while prices were only vaguely limited; where the price guidelines were specific, they excluded numerous products. It should come as no surprise that prices since last October have risen substantially, while wages have been effectively controlled. Thus workers have borne the hardship of this inflation.

Rather than wages, consider only the inflation effect of the zooming interest rate. It was thought at one time that raising interest rates and tightening the money supply would automatically curtail inflationary pressures. The idea was that by keeping money tight, it would become too expensive to borrow and business would slow down; when business slows down, people lose jobs, demand slows down, and inflation is thus brought to a standstill. Nixon tried it, and with OPEC's additional help, by twice doubling its oil prices back in 1973, we plunged into the terrible recession of 1974-75.

Stagflation is a different cat; it chases its own tail. Unemployment becomes a cause of inflation rather than an effect, and the higher inflation causes still more unemployment. Around and around they spiral, ever faster, ever higher.

In our panic to halt inflation, we may be stampeded into

programs which have the ring of righteousness but which actually can toll the bell of ruination. Foremost among proposed solutions is balancing the federal budget. This has the force of a reasonable idea, yet the facts say otherwise. For example, the rate of Germany's budget deficit compared to her GNP is fully three times the rate of our deficit while her inflation rate is less than one-half of ours. Another example: Gerald Ford left office with a staggering $60 billion deficit, but the inflation rate was 4.6 percent. Jimmy Carter's next budget will have cut more than two-thirds of that deficit and we will be down to about $16 billion, but our inflation is more than twice as high. In 1933 Roosevelt was advised by various sages to balance the budget and had he followed their counsel, the country would never have recovered from the great depression.

Limiting interest rates and controlling credit

Last year at this time the prime rate was 11¾ percent, compared to about 6½ percent two years earlier in 1977. General Motors itself can hardly borrow money at that rate. Even large companies have to maintain bank balances that raise their borrowing costs to more than 15 percent, and, of course, small business has to pay even more. I make no claim to being an economist and I wish one of them would explain to me, clearly and simply, how a Mount Everest interest rate will control this inflation. It cannot bring food costs down. It will have no effect whatsoever on OPEC prices, which are up 2000 percent since 1973. High interest rates can only push the cost of housing even farther out of reach of workers and everyone else. As a cure for stagflation high interest rates make no sense to me; only bankers gain.

Interest rates must come down. The Federal Reserve Bank must lower the discount rate and all the states should maintain their present definitions of usury. Hand in hand with lower interest rates must come controls regulating credit. Banks must be encouraged by allocation rules to lend more home mortgage money. Consumers must be discouraged from spending by higher down payment requirements and shorter pay-back periods.

Wage and price controls

Our inflation is a new beast whose nature is to feed upon itself. Most Americans favor strong wage and price controls as the obvious, sensible way both to halt spiraling prices and to quiet the panic. This perception of events causes businesses to raise prices in expectation of higher costs and persuades consumers to stock up or buy ahead to beat the price increases they know are coming. Most business people expect such controls; only economists have been generally opposed, until the inflation rate hit an annualized 18 percent.

The AFL-CIO has long urged a wide-ranging controls program, not only for the usual "wage and prices," but to cover all prices and all forms of income: profits, dividends, rents, interest rates, executive bonuses, professional fees.

Contrary to popular reportage, short-term controls have worked very well. Truman's 30-month wage-price freeze during the Korean War, with mandatory ceilings, dropped the rate at which prices advanced from 5.8 percent down to 0.4 percent. Kennedy's worked only partially, because they were voluntary, but they did slow down the rate. Nixon's four-phase controls was sabotaged by OPEC's quadrupling the price of oil in late 1973, shooting up the rate from 3.8 to 12.2 by 1975. In the recent period, energy prices are the major cause of our inflationary pressures and need forceful attention.

D.

Energy: Engine Of Inflation

Columbia University, June 14, 1979.

At the heart of our troubles lie the sudden skyrocketing cost of oil and our desperate need for this expensive oil. It has not merely doubled or quadrupled in price since 1973; we do not even have a word for the rise—from $2 a barrel in 1973 to upwards of $40 today. The price has soared 15 to 20-fold.

Without doubt, controls on oil and natural gas prices must be continued or reinstated. There is no current evidence that letting oil prices rise geometrically has encouraged increased production; on the contrary, it seems that hoarding has taken place in hopes of future higher prices. In fact, the oil companies themselves tell us there is not much more oil to be discovered. If the world is, in fact, rapidly running out of petroleum, we will only bankrupt ourselves unless we put a lid upon the price of what is left of it. A government oil-purchasing commission must be established so that a single legal authority negotiates with OPEC. This body would also allocate all supplies.

There are two courses to take and they must be taken together. We must conserve: reduce demand. At the same time we must convert: find other forms of energy.

We now know much about how to conserve and it is by far the easiest, safest, cheapest route. For example, mild insulation—not major installations—in every U.S. house is estimated to save two-thirds of all the oil being imported from all the Arab countries plus Iran. This is called retrofitting, meaning to upgrade by adding improvements. We must immediately provide generous tax incentives to get Americans to spend the money for retrofitting. These are not big dollars: For $200 you can buy attic insulation kits in Puget sound, in the cold Northwest, cutting fuel use 22 percent. In Portland, Oregon, not a warm place, $981 worth of standard insulation devices saves fully one-half the fuel costs.

Dr. Robert Williams of Princeton has aptly called this "drilling for oil and gas in our buildings." He and Dr. Marc Ross of Michigan University liken retrofitting to buying oil at $10 a barrel instead of $40.

The conservation measures of which I speak would pose no hardship, require no sacrifice, and very often cost not a penny. This winter, for example, we set our thermostat at 68° and sometimes lower, and not only saved money but felt better. IBM saved $90 million in energy from 1974 to 1977 and, of this savings $60 million cost no money. It came not from space-age hi-jinks but from down-home touches like turning off lights, shutting down equipment, plugging air leaks. Small tricks add up. If everyone installed the new hot-water-saving shower heads, that alone would remove the need for two new power plants.

Commerical places can save about 8 percent on their energy costs by co-generation, recirculating the heat given off in their old buildings. A brand-new 20-story skyscraper has been built in the frigid city of Toronto, Canada, without a conventional furnace. The warmth comes entirely from heat given off by lighting, office equipment, and workers.

Drilling for oil in your own gas tank

Some conservation measures will take laws and public financing. The place to begin is with transportation because cars, trucks and buses use more than half the oil burned in the U.S.A. If people had a cheap alternate way to get about, they would certainly drive cars less. The reason New York State uses the least amount of energy per person is the fabulous subway system in New York City, used by 3½ million riders a day. We in labor favor the development and tax support of every form of mass transit.

Autos alone, in fleets and privately owned, burn up most of the oil used for transportation. If cars could run on half the gas they used to use, we would save about 25 percent of all the oil we need, a fantastic amount. The Energy Policy and Conservation Act of 1975 has set a target of 27.5 miles per gallon as the average mileage of each manufacturer's line.

At the same time as we conserve energy, we must seek alternate forms and renewable forms. Oil is not only too expensive to burn, but it is a rapidly depleting mineral. Nuclear energy, once so full of promise, has also turned out to be expensive and may be unacceptable; waste disposal problems multiply the costs and cause other problems and present generators may be unsafe. The government must accelerate the search for energy sources: solar, fusion, wind, tidal, geothermal, water-falls, gasahol, synthetic fuels, coal liquification and gasification—in short, every avenue must be explored.

Whatever replaces gasoline in the U.S. auto saves the world astounding amounts of petroleum: U.S. cars alone consume one-ninth of all the oil burned up around the globe every single day! We hear of gasohol, alcohol, synfuels, of hydrogen as a fuel. One labor group supported by the ILG has been investigating the way to retrofit autos right now using methane instead of gasoline. Methane can be made by gasifying coal and even from garbage.

These technologies are still experimental and some are expensive, while conservation techniques are known, reasonable, pollution-free and often no-cost. If every homeowner insulated and installed storm windows, if every car buyer simply chooses a car next time that goes twice as far on a gallon of gas than his or her previous model—from just these decisions, millions of barrels of oil would not have to be imported. Our payments abroad would be balanced, the dollar would be stronger, inflation would deflate. We would have more real dollars fattening our wallets.

All other problems may seem pale compared to these. Yet we should remember that even before the energy crisis and inflationary developments, the United States was not a paradise for everyone. There is a long unfinished agenda waiting to be addressed.

E.
New Labor Legislation: Doesn't Labor Deserve An Even Break?

Columbia University, June 14, 1979.

A chill has spread over the U.S. workplace; a climate has been created in which the labor movement is finding it difficult, even dangerous, to grow. We seem to be returning to the mean stormy days of earlier times.

This must be reversed. New national labor legislation is required. The Right to Work laws, which fairly should be renamed "Right to Work For Less laws," are state statutes. Bad as they are, they handicap unions most only after a union succeeds in signing an agreement with an employer. Something still remains to be done about the delaying tactics and illegal actions of corporations designed to prevent organizing. Laws must give remedy to workers who have been unfairly treated in their workplaces.

For example, an employer who discharges a worker for trying to organize a union is acting illegally. Nevertheless, it will routinely take two to three years for the wrong to be remedied and for back pay to be received. On occasion, it has taken longer than 25 years! New legislation is needed so the worker can be speedily returned to the job. A law with teeth would bar guilty employers from government contracts for a stated time and would give abused workers double back pay for time out of work.

For its part, labor must organize more of the unorganized.

Historically, skilled tradespeople formed unions, then miners, longshoremen, and workers in manufacturing industries. But almost imperceptibly, except for agriculture, the United States has changed from having a majority of its workers engaged in manufacture to an economy in which more than two-thirds of our workers make a living not producing food or commodities but rather waiting on tables, selling stocks, driving busses—in the service sector.

The United States must re-industrialize. Besides, unions must seek out the more than 50 millions who now have nothing to say about their wages and nothing to say about their working conditions. They work at the whim and fancy of their bosses with no job protection and probably a grim future: Fewer than 1 in 10 will ever collect a full, private pension and so will live out their old age in the poverty of a Social Security income.

When workers reach out to each other to join hands and hearts in union, all of society benefits. Teachers, who bargain collectively for small classroom sizes so they can teach better, improve the schools for everyone. Nuclear workers, who fight for safer work stations, bring us all cleaner air and water. Workers with decent pay checks are the backbone of our consumer economy.

Improved labor legislation, giving workers a better opportunity to decide about joining a union, won the majority of Congress but lost by only one vote in the filibuster mounted to defeat it. Labor did not get beat; it was the democratic process that got kicked in the face. We must fight for new law again. No other free, democratic, industrialized nation places such obstacles in the path of its labor.

F.

Tax Justice And The Inequitable Distribution Of Wealth

Columbia University, June 14, 1979.

The U.S. labor movement struggled long and hard for an equitable progressive income tax. But our income tax system has become progressively non-progressive and we haven't been able to cope with this. Every attempt at tinkering with the tax system results in a more regressive bill.

In the last three decades, our corporations' share of taxes paid out has plunged from almost a third of the federal government's total tax receipts in 1946 down to only 15 percent in 1978. At the same time, the Social Security tax, a regressive tax about half of which is paid by workers, has soared from 8 percent to 31 percent. Since World War II, the federal tax burden has been steadily shifting from the corporation to the working person.

We pay more as workers than our fair share, more than we ought to pay compared with the other elements in this society. When you work from Monday through Friday and you get your week's pay, the tax collector was there before you. He put his arm into your pay envelope and took out what he considers to be his share. There are millions of Americans, not weekly wage earners, to whom that does not happen. There are weekly wage earners, top executives, whose total wage is more than what they get in the pay envelope. They have extras, expense allowances and very valuable perquisites of office. They don't pay a penny tax on those things and a lot of it is our fault.

We all know about sales taxes. It is a nice, easy way to collect a few pennies, isn't it? I remember when I was a young business agent representing garment workers in the northeast part of the country, the State of Massachusetts needed some money to balance the budget. Someone came up with the idea of a sales tax. He went around saying: "You know, it's nice and easy. You buy something for a dollar, all you do is throw a penny on the counter and you've paid the tax. After all, what's a penny? We can all spare that." And so we went to sleep. We did not get up and say: "Now *wait* a second. This is nice and easy, but it doesn't sound quite right." We let the lawyers, the accountants, the bankers and the politicians who were not our friends talk us into it. We had a sales tax. Then I went into the store—and I wasn't making much money—and I bought something for a dollar and I threw a penny on the counter. Right behind me followed the fellow who owned a big factory; he bought the same item—put a dollar down and threw a penny on the counter. The tax system in America was based on one's ability to pay, on the theory that those of us who had the least should pay the least, and those of us who could afford to pay more should pay more. That was the American way. All of a sudden, here I am paying my penny and there is the rich man paying his penny.

The next year, they needed a few dollars more in Massachusetts so they raised the sales tax from one percent to two percent, then from two to three, from three to four, from four to five, from five to six. Now it's seven percent! In New York State, it's seven and eight! Look at what has happened. The garment worker who makes $4,500 and $5,000 a year goes up to buy some item, throws six or seven pennies on the counter. A lawyer, a doctor, the businessman or the fellow who owns the store in the community—he follows right after, buys the same item, throws the same six or seven pennies on the counter. The Federal government does it with excise taxes that are on almost everything you and I buy. Some day, if you buy a new car, look at that little line where it says "Federal excise tax." That is a fancy name for sales tax.

Beyond taxes is a more basic problem, where I am hopeful the American trade union movement may have some serious impact. This is the question of the maldistribution of income and wealth in our country. I believe, along with many political philosophers, that people are poor in this country because some industries pay subminimal wages and rely upon the rest of us to subsidize their working poor. In 1977, the lowest-paid 20 percent of workers in this country, the lowest one-fifth, earned only 5.2 percent of total income. The top one-fifth, meanwhile, earned 41.5 percent of the income.

We do have transfer payments; we have social welfare legislation; we have the achievements of the unions; we have businessmen who are much less parochial than they used to be. So one might reasonably assume that income distribution in this country would be a lot more even than it was in the past. In the last 30 years, however, the lot of the lowest one-fifth of workers in the United States has improved by only two-tenths of one percent. In 1977 they earned, as I noted, 5.2 percent of the total income. Thirty years earlier in 1947, they had 5.0 percent of the income. If they continue to add two-tenths of one percent each 30 years, everyone alive today will be long dead before the bottom 20 percent of our population has anything approaching a semblance of equity.

G.

Military Strength: Might Not Myth

Trilateral Commission,
Washington, D.C., June 112, 1978, and
Columbia University, June 14, 1979.

All of us care about how the government spends our tax

money. We pay attention to government spending, on the federal, state or local level. Much still remains to be done in our economy, but though the United States is a rich nation, we cannot necessarily accomplish everything we want or even everything we feel we need. With the available resources, we must match our needs and desires against what is attainable. Thus we are forced to make choices. We may not be able to have all the highways we want, nor finance all the cancer research we want unless we recognize that we must give up something else to get them.

In the best of all worlds the thing to give up would be guns and tanks. Everyone knows that guns and tanks do not produce more wealth. Jobs are created, it is true, but not nearly the number made in any other line of work. Flying a training mission only burns up and blows up precious resources.

After World War II we in the United States eagerly disbanded the greatest war machine ever known so that we might pursue peace. We soon rediscovered that the Soviet Union was still bent on world dominion by any means. In those years they were too weak for military adventurism; they seemed to rely on their rhetoric alone to subvert other nations. But it is 30 years later and for the past decade, Russia has been outspending us $2 to our every $1 in weapons and research. Their merchant fleet has trebled, ours is down almost 60 percent. The Soviets now have a standing army of 4.4 million to our 2.1 million; theirs has grown by 800,000 since 1961, ours has shrunk by 400,000. We might discount the millions the Soviets keep in their armed forces to subjugate their own people and the people of Eastern Europe, and to police their endless border with China; that still leaves an awesome army, free for adventurism. Their total military budget is $162 billion to our $124 billion but that represents about 12 percent of their total output to our 6 percent.

Why do they do it? What are their intentions? How do we respond to the threat? Neither pieties nor invectives nor warnings will keep the Soviet bear at bay. Only strength, perceived and visible, is a deterrent. Only might, not myth, will protect us.

Our military costs are about 23 percent of our government spending, which means simply that we must postpone other expenditures. It is a horrendously high figure, but upon it depends the continued freedom of millions. The United States carries a high burden to protect the free world. Germany and Japan are prevented by the peace treaties from spending more than a trifle on their arms. Perhaps the time is here for us to trust their 30-year-old vigorous democracies and to call upon them to assume the burden of their own defense and in the process reduce our own military commitments.

The ease with which Soviet imperialism has pursued its global aggression under the cover of detente has shaken up many of us. We must face the problem of rejuvenating NATO to make it a more effective deterrent to Soviet aggression. It is most urgent that practical steps be taken very soon to overcome the doubts and difficulties in the North Atlantic Treaty Organization.

Napoleon once said, "Give me an alliance against which to fight." NATO, which has served as a truly effective instrument of peace, is an alliance and therefore not free from certain inherent dangers; but such dangers need not be harmful if they are met forthrightly, if they are not allowed to fester. Only those who flee from reality will deny that NATO has displayed a feeble will. Too many of its members have not been sufficiently aroused by the grave Soviet threat to Western Europe's integrity, freedom and way of life. All NATO members must pitch in to revitalize morale and restore unity of action as well as aim. Even the smallest NATO member must desist from lending aid and comfort to any power or to the pawn of any superpower engaged in aggression or subversion, whether in Latin America, Africa or the Middle East.

For our part, we in the U.S. must begin to exert strong leadership. Geography and the destiny of history have made the U.S. the only power capable of providing the decisive resources for effective leadership to the great Atlantic Alliance. It must be frankly admitted that recent years have witnessed a decline of U.S. credibility abroad. There would be nothing gained by allocating blame for our past failures of will. Our common task is to end the dangerous drift. We must eliminate points of friction. We must drop the illusion that somehow things will right themselves. Geographically, NATO protects the North Atlantic, but as an instrument of peace, freedom and decency, its aspirations are global and indivisible, and its course of action therefore must not reek of contradictions.

We must rouse ourselves, in view of the escalating conventional and nuclear military strength of the Soviets and their use of surrogate armies in Africa and the Middle East, all of which are geared to aggression.

The defense of the free world from this aggression demands our political will and, unfortunately, a good deal of our economic wealth as well. Who among us can fairly say that the burden is not worth the price of liberty?

H.

Labor Is All-Out For The Equal Rights Amendment

Conference on passage of the ERA, the White House, Washington, D.C., February 11, 1980.

For a long time the American labor movement has been aware of the discrimination against women in our society both as workers and as citizens. Many, many inequities have the force of law as well as custom behind them. The passage of the Equal Rights Amendment will dispose of those written into the laws of our land.

We in labor may not have taken the lead we should have in

INTERNATIONAL
LADIES
UNION
ERA
United Industrial Wukers of
EQUAL RIGHTS
FOR
WOMEN

efforts to ameliorate this problem. In truth, the fault does not lie with ourselves alone but rather in our communities. The AFL-CIO reflects the thoughts, the mores, the habits—and even the prejudices—of the communities from which we draw our members. We lead our members and are lead by them.

There are very compelling reasons why we must redouble our activities. Somewhat more than 50 percent of women of working age are in the work force, yet only one working woman in ten belongs to a trade union. The huge majority have nothing to say about their wages and working conditions. Not only do they work at the whim and pleasure of their bosses as do unorganized men, but they confront obstacles and difficulties by virtue of their gender.

Through our collective bargaining agreements, we in organized labor have been attempting—successfully, for the most part—to eliminate the differences in wage schedules and seniority rights. In the factories, in the mines and in the mills where we have bargaining rights, we have accomplished much. But there is much yet to be done and we intend to do it.

Perhaps the easiest part of our objective is to achieve equal pay for equal work, an area in which we are progressing by leaps and bounds. But there are other, more stubborn problems we see ahead. Some I confront as head of my own union, the ILGWU. One is the fact that several industries and several areas of employment have become known as "women's work."

Average earnings and benefits in these jobs usually are far lower than earnings and benefits in work situations filled by—or even reserved for—male workers; women earn, on the average, some $100 a week less than men. We have a deep obligation to bring about a reasonable and just mix of opportunity so that an industry like our garment trade, for example, where 85 percent of the work force are women, no longer will be down in the lowest 20 to 25 percentile of industrial wages in our country.

Conversely, there are very few women in those industries where workers enjoy optimum wages and conditions. Here, women are generally in clerical capacities or light, labor-intensive work. There are such great disparities in earnings that men working in what have been commonly known as "male crafts" can be earning twice as much or more as women employed within the same general area in what is known as "women's work." In garment shops, this is beginning to change; the highest-paying jobs, which in the past went to men, have been opening up to women.

The whole concept of equal pay for comparable worth is a novel one and extraordinarily difficult to put into practice. For example, a highly-skilled and experienced woman operating a sewing machine to stitch a complicated dress will be paid far less than a man or woman whose only responsibility all the livelong day is to look at the blinking lights of an automated machine and call for help when the warning buzzer signals trouble. Overcoming this inequity is fraught with problems. It goes against conventional wisdom to set wage rates according to fair principles rather than competitive market relationships.

The challenges to our union movement are many. We must break out from the strictures by which many industries seem bound, where certain jobs with superior wages and conditions are set aside for men. We must raise the wages and benefits of low-paid industries where women are in preponderance, where they are regarded as a source of cheap labor. We must strive to break down the barriers to opportunities, to remove all hurdles to better wages and working conditions.

In addition to what we can do through industrial action, we must work to get laws guaranteeing a workplace free of discrimination, particularly of sex discrimination. Thousands of laws affect women adversely. There are laws that prohibit women from working in certain jobs, that establish dual pay schedules. All of them will be wiped out in one blow with the passage of the ERA.

We pledge to you all of our interest, all of our ability, all of our effort to help persuade the legislators in those states that have not yet ratified the Equal Rights Amendment—particularly Florida, Illinois and Missouri, states that should have done so long ago. We will help to persuade them to do the eminently right thing. You can count on us.

two

Corporate Responsibility

The American Assembly of Collegiate Schools of Business, New Orleans, La., May 24, 1979.

> To some 600 deans of schools of business attached to U.S. universities.

During the last decade several serious problems in our national life have boiled over. I want to examine the role that large corporations play as the source of some of these problems and the ways these enterprises might provide solutions.

There are fully two million corporations in this country, yet the top 500 of them produce 60 to 70 percent of all the profit earned. Moreover, while only 5 percent of the establishments in the private sector employ more than 50 people each, their workers add up to nearly half our labor force. Many corporate budgets exceed those of several individual states in the United States, and, indeed, of many countries.

The market power exhibited by these corporate concentrations must be examined closely. Their very capacity for good and evil commands our attention. No longer should corporations operate with minimum oversight. They have become social, quasi-public institutions; their decisions affect not only individuals but entire communities. They must be responsible to those whose day-to-day lives will be changed.

I see this responsibility as follows: to produce plentifully competitively and profitably those products our people need and want, with due regard to the health, safety, moral standards and social improvement of us all, as well as the expansion of our democratic spirit. That is a tall order for what was once solely an economic unit. But a determined effort must be made to expand corporate responsibility. Some enterprises have already demonstrated a capacity to meet these challenges.

Environmental protection is one such challenge. We cannot court grave illness today and tomorrow caused by companies that foul the air, poison the water and carelessly dispose their toxic wastes. Ours is a fragile planet; we must all cooperate to keep it a garden for all time.

U.S. corporations must do their part to revitalize our cities. The core of every single one of our old great cities is rotting and needs rehabilitating. Tens of thousands live there, many now without work, perhaps without hope. They can be fed and housed at public expense, kept alive—with little concern for decent or humane treatment, but at least alive. Welfare alone, however, will never solve this problem. Our huge corporations have the right and duty to expand into new and exciting places, but they cannot be permitted to abandon or ignore older areas. They must serve America's needs in addition to their own. They must help rehabilitate the cities that have made this country great. Local communities and the federal government must provide some means to remind corporations of this responsibility.

Corporations nearly always plan shutdowns far in advance and they should be required to make those plans public early so that responses can be developed and solutions found. I think we can no longer permit members of a board of directors, located thousands of miles from a community in which they employ 3,000 or 4,000 workers, to make a cold-turkey decision to shut down a plant. That decision, though based on hitherto acceptable economic theory, creates great trauma and despair, not alone for workers and their families but for every member of the abandoned community. Ultimately, the decision also takes its economic toll from the fortunate ones in the new location who must help pay for the cost of increased food stamps, welfare, perhaps even crime and alcoholism caused by the relocation.

I would suggest that corporations be required to provide a community impact statement before any decision to close down can be carried out. That statement should be looked at by an inter-agency committee composed of representatives of the U.S. Treasury and the Departments of Labor and Commerce. It should consider the effects of a plant shutdown on jobs and on the tax base.

Many approaches are possible. Some are already being tried. For example, if it is not economically feasible for the corporation to continue its operation, perhaps workers could be retrained before the business goes under, and another company found to come in and use the new skills. Perhaps some cooperative undertaking might result in jobs for workers in a community with no other employment. The government might subsidize in some limited way the operation of that plant.

Over the past years many U.S. corporations have evolved into multinational corporations. We must pay far more attention to the activities of these U.S. multinational corporations. There has been some romantic talk about them, but little fundamental research or real discussion on the effect of these international giants upon our nation's economy: on our employment, on our manufacturing base, on our tax policies, on our competitive position in the world, on our failure to spend adequate funds on research and development. Consider only one point: U.S. corporations have often failed to reinvest in the United States the profits they made here, yet at the same time they have poured tremendous amounts of U.S. capital into overseas countries. In the last two decades, while at home we holler about the "shortage" of capital, these multinationals have become the third largest economic force in Europe. If we are to increase our productivity and provide more jobs in our own country, it is vital that we invest more capital here.

We must also take a hard look at the virtually unchallenged decisions of boards of directors and corporate executives who set up plants overseas. They sell and lease their technology; in some cases, the high "Cadillac" technology not yet in place here in this country can be found in factories abroad. Workers in this country are concerned about the export of their jobs. They say it simply and clearly just like that—"the export of our jobs." Their jobs have flown off, gone overseas. When academicians and corporate officers meet to talk about these matters, they do not use such down-to-earth phrases. Instead, they talk of the "transfer of capital and technology," as though they were transferring objects unconnected to real, live human beings.

If any act can be described as worse than robbing the United States of jobs, it is the way American multinational corporations are wheeling and dealing with non-market economies like Russia and China, building turnkey plants. This is total irresponsibility. Utter immorality. Low-paid workers—sometimes slave workers—are trained along with the authoritarian supervisors who are to take over the operation of these plants; U.S. corporations then agree to take back the products to the U.S. market as payment for the erection of the plant and the training of its exploited workers. What could be more encouraging to despotic regimes overseas, or more devastating to their valiant dissidents, or more destructive to the interest of the United States?

I do not know whether General Motors has set up the plant in Poland for which they were negotiating. I do know there has been a terrible rush into Red China to accommodate the Red Chinese. In the ILG we know of a singularly outrageous case. One manufacturer of expensive jeans has built a garment factory for a commune in China, in barter for which the workers will be paid coolie wages by their government for five years. No wages from the importer for five whole years! Adding to this shame, the labels, sewn in Red China, will read "Made in Hong Kong." This is the nature of our competition: U.S. corporate carpetbaggers go overseas to seek such opportunities for exploitation and bring those products into the U.S.A.

I dread to think what will happen to the U.S. market, to the U.S. worker, when more U.S. corporations begin to trade with the People's Republic of China. Consider the unfair competition that many U.S. corporations will face. We will sell China our highest technology and to pay for it, inexperienced and destitute Chinese workers will seek to flood the U.S. market with textiles and clothing.

In addition to regulating imports, there must be proper safeguards over the concentration of larger and larger amounts of capital at home. In the past, corporations grow ever bigger through merger and consolidation, or through buying up a larger share of market power to reduce or eliminate the competition in their particular field. But in the last several years they have acquired companies totally unrelated to their product lines or markets. These take-overs should trouble us. Formerly, large corporations were concerned only with market concentration; now their aggregate concentration turns them into conglomerates, ballooning larger and ever larger. Their divisions trade among themselves and close off part of the market to other competition, thus diminishing free enterprise.

We must also ask if legal judgments made in corporate offices should be permitted to transcend morality. Hundreds of corporations have acknowledged bribes, kickbacks and inflated commissions given in the process of selling U.S. goods and services to customers overseas. In the last decade we have come to learn not only about the political Watergate as it wormed its way into the very core of our democratic being, but also about business Watergate as it resulted in the disclosure of corporate graft and corporate illegality at home and abroad.

I know how fervently people with goods and services seek to sell them in the pursuit of profit. I know what it means to meet competition. Such actions are wrong, but are done anyway to get business; everybody else is doing it and you are judged and rewarded on your sales performance, not your ethical performance. Such problems raise the question of corporate governance and accountability. There are no easy answers. Business will have to depend on those among you with a sense of morality to prevent ours from becoming a cynical, venal era. Corporate executives are not immoral people just because they have chosen to become executives. Each of us in a position of authority needs help in arriving at workable solutions that are also ethical.

There should be fuller financial disclosure requirements for corporations, equal to what is demanded of labor unions in this country. Salaries, perquisites, expense accounts, loans, cars, stock options—unions are required to report all of these if they are present for employees who earn $10,000 or more. Yet corporations are required to disclose these matters only for their boards of directors or a few senior corporate officials.

I believe in free, democratic, competitive capitalism and it follows that I would like to see our capitalism even more free, more democratic and more competitive. We might start by changing the makeup of many boards of directors. A board of directors empowered by law and custom with the right to set policy and direct the affairs of the corporation should not be overloaded with input from people hired to carry out the day-to-day functions of the business. Other opinions, now lacking among most of our corporate boards, must be heard. I do not, however, normally favor union representation on corporate boards, as is done in Germany and England. In my view, workers on such boards begin to be co-opted by management's problems and could neglect their own. Managers should manage and then workers should sit down with them to collectively bargain for their share of the results of management efficiency and worker productivity.

Corporate boards tend to be filled with members who may have difficulty in acting independently because they have conflicting interests. When a banker sits on the board of a company to whom he lends money, when someone who supplies materials sits on the board of the company that buys them, a chill stunts the expression of independent thought and action. Of 130 corporations that had 25 percent of all the corporate assets in this country, there were 530 direct interlocks and about 12,000 indirect interlocks. With a reduction of direct and indirect interlocks, greater competition will be assured. We must change, and change quickly, situations where two people who are competitors sit on the board of a third company, or where one person sits on the boards of two competitors.

When corporate power is great and becoming greater,

when it is concentrated in fewer and fewer hands, when corporate decisions affect our lives so intimately, it is important to remember that the greatness of a nation—its purpose, its cultural and scientific eminence, the tenor of its daily life—is ultimately manifested through the individuals who are the living carriers of its values.

It is reassuring to find that our leading educators, entrusted with the care of young and future management leaders, are grappling with these problems. I have no idea what methods or principles will evolve as solutions. To paraphrase Sir Thomas More: Suppose you cannot, as you wish, eradicate vice of long standing. Do not despair on that account and abandon your post. Rather redouble your efforts and what you cannot turn to right, you must make as little wrong as your efforts will permit.

I have touched on many issues. Let me conclude with the critical one. The mission of the U.S. trade union movement today, as it has ever been, is to contribute its best thinking, its finest efforts and all its strength to a free and prosperous United States, whose hallmark must be equal justice for all. We must not accept the trappings of democracy without providing economic security for all of our people as well as the opportunity for political freedom. That has been our goal from our beginnings. It continues to be our objective and our highest aspiration.

To this end may I hope for the active support and full participation of people from all sectors of our economy and our community. None of us possesses the revealed truth. Together we may create an acceptable fellowship of citizenry.

End Note

The editors wish to express their gratitude to the many persons who helped in the preparation of this book. In the ILGWU New York office, Alice Christiano's gracious assistance and Gladys Scher's cheerful, dependable work are much appreciated. Walter Mankoff, assistant director of research, confirmed endless statistics. Meyer Miller, editor of *Justice*, the ILG's newspaper, and managing editor Dwight Burton ferreted out many of the pictures. Assistant president Gus Tyler's writings and advice were essential sources. Miriam Sluchan's flawless files and encyclopedic knowledge of Chaikin's activities, interests and friends over many years were a most valuable resource. Dr. Lazare Teper, ILGWU director of research, spent many hours attempting to educate us in the often arcane and still-puzzling practices of both international trade and national labor relations. Whatever clarity the editors' remarks display is due in large measure to his care.

Outside the ILG family there were many whose contributions were decisive. We extend our grateful appreciation to Judge Jack B. Weinstein who was among the first to encourage us in this work and who then brought a writer's ear to the manuscript, giving unstintingly of his time. Al Romm provided an editor's guidance and constant support. Bertha Hartman's meticulous reading and Karen Chaikin's fastidious analysis were invaluable. The contributions of Judy Bardacke and Sidney Shapiro were crucial. Linda Aumick, reference librarian at Middletown's Thrall Library, was continually helpful.

We particularly applaud our publisher, Matilda Gocek. May all who wish to give birth to books have the good fortune to fall into such steadfast and competent hands.

Rosalind Bryon Chaikin New York, N.Y.	Ethel Grodzins Romm Middletown, N.Y.

Acknowledgements

Index

Ackley, Gardner 189
Advertising, television and radio 136
American Federation of Labor-Congress of Industrial Organizations (AFL-CIO) 33, 39, 43, 51, 82, 100, 101, 117, 135, 152, 158, 161
Advanced Nations Conference 53
African-American Labor Council 157
Aliens, illegal (see Workers undocumented)
Amaike, Seije 56
Amalgamated Clothing and Textile Workers 65, 67
American Assembly of Collegiate Schools of Business 215
American Can Company 93
American Immigration and Citizenship Conference 148
American Institute for Free Labor Development (AIFLD) 157, 175, 179
Anderson, John 5
Anti-Nazi Non-Sectarian League 100
Appalachia 149
Appleton, Shelley 157
Argentina 11, 15, 39, 43, 156, 171
Arms production 208
Asian Regional Organization (ARO) 51
Australia 11, 15

Balance of Trade 13, 202
Baltimore, Md. 22, 23
Bangladesh 112
Belgrade 161
Belguim 112
Bicknell, Indiana 30
Bloomingdale's 22
Blumenthal, W. Michael 62
Brandeis, Louis 106
Brazil 9, 11, 14, 157
British National Steel Corporation 84
Brown, Irving 51
Brown, Lester R. 15
Brzezinski, Zbigniew 5
Bukovsky, Vladimir 161, 165
Bureau of Labor Statistics 93

Calcutta cloth 112
California 27
Canada 15, 51, 63, 111, 201
Callaghan, James 189
Carter, Pres. Jimmy 5, 43, 65, 73, 77, 168, 171, 179, 180, 181, 189, 194, 198
Chicago, Ill. 110
Chile 156, 171, 173-178
China, People's Republic of 48, 54, 69, 77, 84, 156, 209, 218
Class struggle 131
Codes, trade 77, 78, 82-84
Collective bargaining 98, 117, 124-132, 138, 176, 212, 220
Collective bargaining, arbitration 106
Columbia University at Arden House, Harriman, NY 27, 119, 124, 187
Committee for Economic Development (CED) 75
Common Market 11
Communications Workers Union of America 107
Communist Party 107
"Comparative advantage" 12, 77, 112, 217
Comparison shopping, men's clothing 23
Comprehensive Employment and Training Act (CETA) 191
Conference on Security and Cooperation in Europe (CSCE) 165
Congressional Record 28
Connecticut 110, 111, garment worker losses in 30
Cornell University, Ithaca, NY 93, 187

Council for International Affairs, Harvard University 37
Council of Economic Advisors 189
Council on Foreign Relations (CFR) 75
Cuba 178
Czechoslovakia 165, 171

Daily News Record 55
Daniels, Wilbur 137
Day care centers 123, 130
Denmark 160
Depression (1929-1932) 192, 195
d'Estaing, Giscard 189
DGB (German labor organization) 56
Domei (Japanese Federation of Labor) 53, 56
Dominican Republic 21
Dubinsky, David vi, 103, 155
Dubrow, Evelyn 137
Dumping, antidumping 11, 17, 77, 83, 84, 85
Duties (see tariffs)

East Germany 165, 171
"Economic hardship" 122
The Economist 14
Education, public 97
Egg Harbor, N.J. 28
Egypt 159
Eisenhower, Pres. Dwight D. 189

El Salvador 21
Energy Policy and Conservation Act of 1975 202
England, See Great Britain
Environmental Protection Agency 127
Equal Rights Amendment (ERA) 100, 210-213
European Trade Union Congress (ETUC) 51

Excelsior (newspaper) 37
Executive Program in Business Administration 27, 119, 124, 187

Fashion Institute of Technology, N.Y.C. 103, 109
Federal Reserve Bank 198
Federal Trade Commission 21
Federal Unemployment Tax Act 130
Florida, garment worker losses in 30
Ford, Pres. Gerald 189, 198
Ford Motor Co. 43
France 34, 51, 62, 84, 112, 156, 160, 189
"Free trade", "free traders" 8-10, 14, 16, 17, 25, 39, 55, 77, 80
Full Employment Act (1946) 123
Furukawa, Tsukasa 54

Gamsakhurdia, Zviad 164
General Agreement on Tariffs and Trade (GATT) 3, 55, 75
General Electric (GE) 82, 129
General Motors 43, 107, 120, 218
Germany 27, 34, 43, 46, 51, 56, 80, 81, 113, 152, 189, 192, 198, 209, 220
Ginzburg, Alexander 164
Gleason, Thomas W. 171, 172
Goldberg, Arthur J. 165, 166, 169
Gompers, Samuel 100
Government purchases, codes on 83, 85
Great Britain 10, 46, 51, 63, 84, 112, 156, 160, 171, 189, 220
Green, Paula 136
Green, William 21
Greenspan, Allen 189
Gross National Product 5, 194
"Group Of Ten" (Dinamicos) 172, 175, 179
"Guest workers" 41, 81
Gurion, Ben 160

Haiti 8, 30

Hammonton, N.J. 28
Harvard Council 37
Health care 98
Health Care Act 131
Health Maintenance Organizations 125
Helsinki Accords (Final Act) 161, 163, 166-169
Holland 34, 112, 160
Hollings, Ernest F. 71
Hong Kong 8, 33, 69, 70, 112, 192, 218
Hopkins, John 61
"Hours" bill 31
House Republican Conference 5
House Ways and Means Committee, Trade Subcommittee 21
Housing for workers 99, 125
Hull, Cordell 72, 79
Humphrey-Hawkins Bill (1979) 123

IBM (International Business Machines) 82, 120, 201
Illegal aliens (see Undocumented workers)
Immigrants to U.S. 104, 149
Immigration and Naturalization Service 148
Import penetration chart 32
Imports (see Regulating imports)
India 19, 112
Indiana, garment worker losses in 29, 30
Inflation 125, 129, 188, 189, 190, 194-200, 202
Inheritance laws 122
Interest rates 198
International Association of Machinists 10
International Brotherhood of Electrical Workers 125
International Confederation of Free Trade Unions (ICFTU) 51, 56, 101, 157
International Labor Organization (ILO) 39, 59, 100
International Labor Press Association (ILPA) 135
International Ladies' Garment Workers' Union (founding) 103, 104; loss of members 135
International Longshoremen's Association (ILA) 171, 172
International Textile, Garment & Leather Workers' Federation (ITGLWF) 157
Iran 200
Ishpeming, Mich. 30
Israel 39, 156, 159
Israeli Federation of Labor (Histadrut) 160
Italy 9, 34, 51, 63, 112, 156, 160

J.C. Penney 111
Japan 4, 6, 7, 11, 22, 34, 45, 46, 51-57, 77, 78, 80, 81, 85, 152, 180, 181, 188, 209
Japan Export Clothing Manufacturers Association (JECMA) 55
Japanese Fed. of Labor (see Domei)
Jewish Labor Committee 100
Johnson, Pres. Lyndon B. 189

Kennedy Round 79
Kentucky 27
Kersten, Otto 56
Kirkland, Lane 51
Knitgoods Local 155   33, 34
Knitgoods Local 190   31, 33, 34
Knitwear 33
Korea 8, 45, 53, 70, 144, 157
Kostrava, Merab 164

Labor Summit 51, 53, 56, 180
Labor Union Leaders Conference 51
Labour Party, England 47
League of Nations 160

228

Loginov, Vadim 165
Logansport, Ind. 29, 31
London Summit 53
Longo, Frank 157
Louisville, Ky. 110
Luxembourg 160

McCracken, Paul 189
Macy's 22
Marshall, Ray 132
Marshall Plan 100
Massachusetts 27, 110, 111, 206, garment worker losses in 30
Master agreements 140
May, William 93
Mazur, Jay 157
Meany, George 165, 168, 172
Medicaid 192
Meir, Golda 160
Mendelsund, Henoch 157
Meshel, Yerucham 160
Mexico 4, 22, 30, 37-43, 142
Michigan, garment worker losses in 30
Minimum wage 41, 48, 118, 123, 128
Minimum wage, Great Britain 47
Ministry of International Trade and Industry (Japan) 54
Mondale, Walter 5, 181
Montgomery Ward 111
Moynihan, Sen. Daniel Patrick 61, 71
Multifiber Arrangements (MFA) 7, 28, 49, 54, 55, 69, 79
Multilateral Trade Negotiations (MTN) 61, 69-72, 75, 77, 78, 82, 85, 87
Multinational corporations 11, 12, 85, 150, 217, 218

Narayanan, P.P. 56
North Atlantic Treaty Organization (NATO) 209, 210
National Association of Manufacturers (NAM) 132
National Federation of Textile Industry Workers Union, Japan (Zensen) 53, 54
National Labor Relations Act 138, Board 93
National Union of Tailors and Garment Workers, Scarborough, England 46, 170
Negative income tax 123
New Deal 192
New Jersey, garment worker losses in 28-30
New York 144, 206
New York Cloak Joint Board 107
Niki-Lu of Miami, Inc. 21
Nixon, Pres. Richard 189, 197, 199
Norway 160
Nuclear energy 202
N.Y. State School of Industrial and Labor Relations, Cornell 93

Occupational Safety and Health Act (OSHA) 69
Ohira, Prime Minister Masayoshi 52, 56, 180
Oil embargo 135, 160
Okun, Arthur M. 189
Organization of Petroleum Exporting Countries (OPEC) 53, 56-58, 77, 197-200
Organizacione Regional Interamericana de Trabajadores (ORIT) 157
Organization for Rehabilitation and Training (ORT) 156, 157
Orlov, Yuri 164
Overseas Private Investment Corporation (OPIC) 85

Pennsylvania 110, 111, garment worker losses in 30
Philadelphia, Pa. 31, 33
Philippines 30, 80, 145

Pinochet, Pres. Augusto (Chile) 171-180
Poland 43, 218
Presidential Classroom for Young Americans 138
Price, Hickman 62
Price and wage controls 198, 199, 200
Prison camps, Russia 162
"Protectionist" 11, 79
Puerto Rico 34, 63, 111, 130

Quotas 7, 62, 67, 73, 85

RCA Corp. 9
Regulating imports (see also Quotas, Tariffs, Trade, Multifiber Arrangements) 5, 33, 53, 80, 218
Relocation, corporate 127, 216, 217
Retrofitting 200, 201
Ricardo, David 10, 12
Right To Work laws 138, 139, 144, 203
Rockefeller Foundation 15
Rockefeller, David 4
Rome 63
Roosevelt, Pres. Franklin D. 100, 192, 198
Ross, Marc 201
Rudenko, Mykola 164
Russia 107, 159, 208-210, 218

Sakharov, Andrei 161, 165, 166, 168, 170
San Francisco, Ca. 110
Scandinavia 80, 81
Scharansky, Anatole 164
Scherer, Julio 37
Schmidt, Helmut 189
Schneider, Edward 157
Schultze, Charles 189
Sears Roebuck 21, 111
Senate Committee on Finance; Trade Subcommittee 61
Shioji, Mr. 53

Siems, Fred 157
Silverman, Jerry 69
Singapore 8, 112
Smith, Michael B. 70
Smoot-Hawley Tariff 72
Social Security tax, benefits 99, 128, 195, 204, 205
Social unionism 91, 93
Solomon, Anthony 5
South Korea 54, 69, 80
Special Representative for Trade Negotiations 25, 26
Stagflation 190, 196, 197
Stein, Herbert 189
Stein Leon 135
Strauss, Robert 65, 67, 70, 71
Strikes 106, 107, 108, 151, 161, 173, 179
Stulberg, Louis 103
Subsidies 83, 84
Sweatshops 104, 142, 143
Sweden 160

Tadanobu Usami 53
Taft-Hartley Act 139
Taiwan 19, 33, 53, 54, 69, 112, 192
Tariffs 11, 17, 25, 26, 31, 39, 61, 62, 67, 69, 70, 71, 72, 77, 84, 85
Tax advantages, corporations 11, 12
Tax credits 11, 87, 191
Tax, corporate 205
Tax, excise 206
Tax, income 98, 205
Tax, sales 205
Telephone Workers Union 107
Teper, Dr. Lazare 26, 27, 61, 64, 70, 72
Thatcher, Margaret 189
Third World countries 14, 15, 16, 17, 39, 41, 47, 48, 57, 80, 81, 85, 118
Tokyo Round 3, 72, 75, 77, 82, 83, 84
Toyotas 33
Trade Act (of 1974) 26, 82
Trade Act (of 1979) 26, 73, 75
Trade Policy Staff Committee 25

Trade, recommendations 16, 17, 85, 86
Trade Union Advisory Committee (TUAC) 51
Transfer pricing 11
Trilateral Commission 4, 207
Truman, Pres. Harry 199
Turkey 81
Tykhyi, Oleska 164
Tyler, Gus 147, 225

Undocumented workers 43, 118, 148, 150, 151
Unemployment 26, 27, 52, 53, 122, 152, 188, 189, 190, 194-199
Unemployment compensation 99, 125, 127, 130, 192
Unemployment, technological 125, 126
Union-free Environment, Committee for 132
Union label 135-137
United Automobile Workers of America 107, 125
United Nations 14, 39, 158
U.S.A. Today 17
U.S. Department of Agriculture 15
United Steel Workers of America 107
Unity House 3, 19
Usami, Tadanobu 53

Vetter, Heinz 55, 56
Vietnam 142
Volkswagons 33
Vote, right to 97
Voting Rights Act 100

Wage comparison charts, international garment worker rates 89; U.S. Two-tier labor system 116
Wage comparisons 117, 119-121
Wages 46, 59, 85, 95, 96, 122, 141, 178, 188, 196, 213

Wages, minimum 47, 48, 99, 118, 123, 128, 131, 147
Warner's Corp. 22
Watergate 219
Weinberg Seminar 93, 187
West Germany 52
White Stag Co. 22
Williams, Robert 201
Women's Issues 129, 210
Workers, unorganized 115, 117, 140-145, 204
Work In America Institute 115
Working poor 121-123
Workmen's Compensation 99
World Confederation of Labor (WCL) 51
World War (1914-1918) 106, 195
World War (1939-1945) 3, 4, 12, 13, 15, 16, 100, 109, 120, 158, 159, 192, 205, 208
Wortman, Sterling 15

Yugoslavia 81, 166

Zenith Corporation 9
Zensen 53, 54
Zionism 39